Connecting with the Cosmos

Nine Ways to Experience the Wonder of the Universe

Donald Goldsmith

SOURCEBOOKS, INC.®
NAPERVILLE, ILLINOIS

Published by Sourcebooks, Inc.
P.O. Box 4410, Naperville, Illinois 60567-4410
(630) 961-3900
FAX: (630) 961-2168
www.sourcebooks.com

Library of Congress Cataloging-in-Publication Data

Goldsmith, Donald.
Connecting with the cosmos: nine ways to experience the wonder of the universe / by Donald Goldsmith.
    p. cm.
    Includes bibliographical references and index.
    ISBN 1-57071-766-1 (alk. paper)
    1. Astronomy—Popular works. I. Title.

QB44.3 .G65 2001
520—dc21

        2001042028

Printed and bound in China
IM 10 9 8 7 6 5 4 3 2 1

Table of Contents

Dedication

To my daughter Rachel,
who encouraged me to learn sky lore,
and to the memory of George R. Bach,
who inspired me to write this book.

Acknowledgments

In writing this book, I have enjoyed receiving information and encouragement from a host of astronomers, friends, and relatives, some of whom have appeared in multiple roles. I would like to thank in particular Kathy and Bruce Armbruster, Dana Backman, Sam Bader, Arnie Berger, Arlene and Pascal Debergue, Aviva and Ken Brecher, Diana and Butler Burton, Richard Cooper, Richard Dreiser, Susan and George Field, June Fox, Andy Fruchter, Carol and Richard Gammon, Marjorie and Victor Garlin, Owen Gingerich, Glenn Goldschmidt, Jane Goldsmith, Paul Goldsmith, Rachel Goldsmith, Amy and George Gorman, Marjorie and Jerry Heymann, Linda and Don Kripke, Ed Krupp, Jon Lomberg, Steve and Sally Maran, Geoff Marcy, Ellen and Larry Marschall, Johanna and Richard Marquis, Craig and Christina Nova, Eleanor and Sandy Orr, Toby Owen, Merrinell Phillips, Paul Sagalyn, Michael Soule, and Sharon and Michael Wynd. It has been a pleasure to work with Deb Werksman, Tressa Minervini, and the other people at Sourcebooks. My agent, Neeti Madan, has once again proven to be a fount of wisdom and support.

Introduction

What Was Lost Yet May Be Found

"You never gain something but that you lose something," wrote Henry Thoreau.

As a society, we have gained, as Robert Pirsig follows this thought, entire empires of understanding, but as individuals we have lost the sense that we belong to something greater than ourselves. The great astronomical discoveries of modern times, together with the loss of our dark nighttime skies, have lead to a serious decrease in our perception of the cosmos. Our ancestors knew the different tracks that the sun takes across the sky, the phases of the moon, the changing cycles of appearance that Venus and the other planets undergo, the details of the alternation of the seasons, and the star patterns that we call constellations. Our great-grandparents and their great-grandparents, and their forebears back in time for one hundred generations and more, knew the phenomena in this short list far better than we do, and found themselves spiritually enriched by this knowledge. Our predecessors in this earthly realm felt a connection to the cosmos that we no longer can, as they saw the sky arching protectively above the Earth. No wonder, then, that all celestial phenomena called for close attention, laden as they were with meaning for human lives below. I claim that we are impoverished as individuals by our lack of understanding, and that we have thrown the baby of skygazing pleasure out with the bathwater of belief in a cosmos made for ourselves.

The longing for cosmic connection remains with us, however. Over the past thirty years, I have attempted to explain astronomy to people in a way that makes stargazing accessible and understandable to anyone. I have found that when my friends, family, students, or acquaintances follow my instructions for observing the phenomena of the sky—without any need for fancy instruments—they typically report that they have enjoyed a profound experience, one that filled them with deep awe and joy. Seeking to make that connection available to as many people as possible, I have written this book, which presents nine types of astronomical observations that anyone can undertake at any time of life, even within the confines of modern civilization and its nighttime lights. The activities described in each chapter range from the short and simple to the longer and slightly more complex. I encourage you to adapt them to your own tastes, but in any case to give them a try. You will find yourself indulging in a fine bit of stargazing, a pastime as old as humanity itself.

I offer just one note of caution. Because bygone generations had deep wells of mythological tradition on which to rely, they named the stars and constellations after mythological figures and found no difficulty in seeing a bear, a bull, a swan, or a pair of twins wherever their elders told them to look. Although all of us know at one mental level that no such figures exist in the sky, the power of myth still leads many people to tell you (as they have told me) that "I never could really enjoy looking at the stars, because I never could see a bear or a bull." To this, I have no rejoinder that would reach the deep, myth-bound part of our psyches that expects to see a bear or a bull; I can only assert that if you accept the fact that there is no real bear or bull, you can proceed to recognize the constellations with ease, and thus to enjoy your sky-watching evenings with a deepening appreciation of what nature hath wrought.

This book presents my simple request: look at the sky and revel in what you see there. Heavenly delights are waiting for you each time the Earth turns. Grasp them and you connect with human passion and the mystery of creation.

Donald Goldsmith

Chapter *One*

Sunset, Sunrise

Clouds covering the sun provide protection for human eyes, which can be immediately damaged by direct sunlight.

Human lives revolve around the sun, our life-giving star. Even though we now have the technology of artificial lighting, which allows us to do whatever we like long after sunset or well before dawn, we continue to follow the sun in its motions through the sky. All but a tiny minority of the six billion people living on Earth awaken at roughly the time that the sun rises above the horizon, break for a midday meal about when the sun reaches its maximum height in the sky, and cease working as the sun goes down. Tied to the sun by its unseen gravitational force, we on Earth wake and sleep in rhythm with the sun's apparent motions. In every culture and locality on Earth, the most fundamental aspect of watching the heavens has consisted of keeping track of the sun. In this chapter, I invite you to participate consciously, as you do unconsciously, every day in this most ancient of astronomical traditions.

Every morning the sun rises in the east, crosses the sky, and then sets in the west as evening begins. Nothing could be more evident to those who inhabit the Earth, and nothing in the sky drew deeper or more protracted attention from our ancestors. Humans belong to a species that seeks explanations for what we observe. Because of this, most societies created myths representing the sun as a god making a journey each day across the sky, and then, hidden from view, traveling beneath the Earth to regain his starting point on the following dawn.

This sun god ruled the heavens, which humans have always regarded as entirely different from the terrestrial realm below. On Earth, all things change, as birth, growth, death, and decay dominate human events. In the sky, celestial objects wheel through the sky, but have always returned, in a cyclical fashion, to their original positions.

In many different cultures, the division between heaven and Earth appears in a series of dualities, including a polarity between male and female, a comparison between order and disorder, and an opposition between mortal and immortal. Our word "horizon" for the demarcation line that separates the sky from the Earth comes from the Greek verb meaning "to divide," reflecting this fundamental division between heaven and Earth. The book of Genesis devotes an entire day to the task of dividing the two. Even today, when we learn that we live on a cosmic speck of dust in a vast universe made of similar stuff, our inner selves tend to deny such an arrant piece of nonsense. As a result, we continue intuitively to regard the sky as a realm entirely different from all things below.

Although the heavens have always seemed eternal and well ordered—or perhaps precisely because they did so—most cultures have worried deeply over the possibility that this order might revert to chaos. If the sun ceased to rise in its majesty at each successive dawn, what would happen to life on Earth? (Still an excellent question, but one that will not become immediately relevant for another five billion years.)

Our predecessors on Earth therefore prayed not only that the sky gods would exercise their powers wisely, but also that the motions of the heavens would remain well ordered. In fact, this very orderliness, observed if not understood, was and is a source of great comfort to us mortals on Earth. Who among us has not felt awed and uplifted by the sight of a glorious sunset, available to everyone, free of charge, on every evening free of a heavy cloud cover?

Activity One:
See the Evening Sun Go Down

With a modest effort, you can join one thousand generations of your forebears in observing the sun as it sets, enjoying the same psychic sustenance that they drew from watching the sun go down to bring on the night. Go to a spot with a good view of the western horizon and prepare to enjoy your experience fully. You must first, as the doctors say, do no harm: remember that you must *never* look directly at the sun while it is high in the sky! You may look directly at the sun with safety *only* when it is close to the horizon—so close that its color changes from normal yellow sunlight to a deep orange or red. At other times, looking at the sun can damage your eyes before you feel any warning signals of pain! Take a minute, then, as the sun makes its way toward your horizon, to admire how our protective atmosphere allows us to watch the sun go down without risk.

If you glance at the sun ten or fifteen minutes before sunset as it approaches the horizon, you will see that its light has grown noticeably dimmer and redder than usual. As the sun nears the horizon, its rays of light must pass through ever-greater amounts of air. This reduces the intensity of sunlight and changes the sun's color. Our life-giving and life-protecting atmosphere forms a thin and fragile shell around our spherical planet. Thin though it may be, this blanket of air screens out the ultraviolet rays produced by the sun, which would otherwise prove fatal to most life on Earth.

When the sun appears high in the sky, sunlight penetrating the atmosphere passes through only a relatively small amount of air. The amount nearly doubles, however, if you observe the sun when it stands above the horizon one-third of the way to the point directly overhead, called the "zenith." A doubling of the amount of air between ourselves and the sun affects the sun's light only slightly, but as the sun's altitude above the horizon continues to decline, a dramatic increase occurs in the amount of air through which the sun's light must pass to reach your eyes.

As the sun sinks toward the horizon, the amount of air between the sun and your eyes rises to ten, twenty, or even forty times the amount of air directly above you! This produces significant effects on the sunlight that we see. Grains of dust floating in the atmosphere scatter in all directions the sunlight that strikes them.

This scattered light, bouncing from the dust motes in the air above you, makes you see the sky lit from within by pale blue light scattered from the sun's rays. In space, with no dust to scatter sunlight, you would "see" only a pitch-black absence of light. As the sun sinks in the west, sunlight encounters ever-greater amounts of air and undergoes ever more scattering, so that diminishing amounts of the sun's light reach you and the sun becomes safe to observe. The dust grains from which the sunlight bounces affect different colors of light by different amounts: they scatter violet and blue light more efficiently than orange and red light. As a result, more red than blue light reaches us from the sun as it sets. This explains the blazing pink on a deep blue background that painters have striven to capture into art from nature.

If you have a clear western horizon, especially at sea, you can observe the sun sink all the way down. By timing the duration of sunset, you will find that the ball of the sun takes about two minutes to disappear, from the time that the horizon cuts the first sliver of sunlight away to the moment when no sun remains. These rank among the most satisfying two minutes available in human life, as you bask in the cosmic order secure (at least we may hope so) in the knowledge that the sun will return to our realm by morning. An especially clear sunset may reveal an elusive "green flash" just after the sun disappears, as our atmosphere bends sunlight into a short, greenish arc of light above the sun's point of disappearance.

Close to sunset, the sun's rays pass through increasing amounts of the atmosphere and therefore scatter more, causing the sun's light to turn red.

WHERE DOES THE SUN SET?

If asked, "Where does the sun rise, and where does it set?" most of us would answer that the sun rises in the east and sets in the west. Not bad as an approximation, but this statement works only as a summary. In days of old, even ordinary members of society knew that on only two days of the year, the spring and fall equinoxes, will the sun rise exactly toward the east and set directly toward the west. Therefore, as you savor the glorious visual appearance of sunset, you should also engage in a simple scientific observation. I ask you to note the location of this sunset along your horizon, and then to try to determine its relationship to the point that lies directly to your west. You can find this western point by using a pocket compass that shows you the north point. From north you can find south in exactly the opposite direction, and west lies halfway between the two in the general direction of the setting sun. If you don't have a compass handy, you can use a road map, which always shows the "compass rose" of north, south, east, and west. You will likely find that certain streets in your community run exactly in an east-west direction, an orientation used in the first cities and never abandoned by city planners. By orienting yourself with respect to one of these east-west avenues, you can find the due west point on the horizon.

Once you have located this point, you should compare it with the position of the setting sun. On most days of the year, you will find that the sun sets either some distance to the north or some distance to the south of due west. Try to estimate how far from due west the sunset occurs, measured in degrees, the angular unit of measurement that fits the situation. You can rely on the fact that 90 degrees specifies the distance on the horizon all the way from due west to due north. Thus, for example, if you see the sun set to the north of west, at one-fifth of the distance around the horizon from due west to due north, you can record that sunset occurred at 18 degrees north of west. The width of your fist, held at your arm's maximum extent, spans about 10 degrees along the horizon, providing another useful unit of angular measurement, the fist-width. Finally, if you hold your outstretched hand at arm's length, the angular distance from the tip of your thumb to the tip of your forefinger equals about 15 degrees. Can you use these body parts to locate the point where the sun sets? Congratulations! By recording the location of this sunset point with respect to due west, you have made a basic astronomical observation, one that ties you to millennia of human history.

By the way, did it surprise you to find that the sun did not set exactly at the due west point? I certainly hope so; from such surprises come increases in knowledge. Pause to enjoy your surprise; ask yourself why you expected the sun to go down precisely to the west; and compare yourself with your great-grandparents' great-grandparents, who knew far more about these matters because they had a far more intimate connection with sunset than we do. Although we cannot regain this intimacy, each of us can deepen our friendship with the sky through activities as straightforward as watching the sunset and sunrise.

Activity Two:
Follow the Sun

We all take pleasure in watching the sun go down; many of us, with somewhat less joy, occasionally watch the sun rise to start the morning. (Forgive me if you are a morning person, able to relax and admire the sun as it rises, and don't forget to celebrate your-self as a person free from some of others' cares and woes.) Few of us watch the sun rise, then wait a few hours to see how high it climbs in the sky, and finally, at the end of the same day, watch the sun as it sets. But we ought to do so at least once in our lives; it enriches the soul.

Consciously noting the sun's path across the sky throughout the course of a day ties you to an ancient activity and takes you back into eras when the sun's different paths through the sky seemed a glorious spectacle, the finest daytime show in the community. The essence of the sun's motion through the sky lies in the fact that its path changes slightly on each successive day. These changes produce the seasons, which governed all activities in premodern communities and continue to exert enormous influences upon our lives.

In modern society, time is precious, so I ask you to perform only once what your forebears did continually: wake before dawn, verify that you have a relatively cloudless morning, and find a spot where you can see the sun rise above the horizon. (The ideal spot would command a view of the horizon to the west as well as the east, so that you can watch the sunset from this same spot.) Then, using the same techniques that you employed at sunset, determine the location of the sunrise point with respect to the point on the horizon directly to your east.

How High Does the Sun Rise?

Next, as the day wears on and lunchtime approaches, try to estimate when the sun rises highest in the sky. Whatever you do, never look directly at the sun! Do not let your enthusiasm overcome your caution, or your eyes will soon regret that you did. The simplest way to keep track of the sun's angular height above the horizon, which astronomers call its altitude (note that they use this word to denote an angular height, rather than a number of feet or miles above the Earth's surface), is to watch the length of your shadow, which decreases to its minimum length as the sun reaches its maximum altitude. (Page 13 shows how to calculate this altitude by having a friend measure the length of your shadow.) You will notice, without a direct gaze, that when your shadow becomes shortest, the sun appears directly above the south point of the horizon. So your shadow, like all others, points directly to the north at "local noon," the moment when your clocks and watches would register 12 noon were it not for civilizing arrangements such as time zones and daylight savings time. At the time of your shortest shadow, the sun lies above the horizon's south point, somewhere along the imaginary line that rises from the due south point, passes directly overhead, and then sinks to the north point on the horizon. Because of time zones and daylight savings time, the sun can cross this meridian line, whose name means "mid-day," as late as 1:30 P.M. By noting the time on your watch when your shadow is shortest, you can determine the difference between "clock time" and "sun time" in your neighborhood.

Comparing the Points of Sunrise and Sunset

If you remain alert through the afternoon and sense the sun's changing position, you will recognize a fundamental fact about the path that the sun takes through the sky. On every day of the year, that path displays a perfect symmetry with respect to the meridian. The sun's trajectory after local noon exactly mirrors that before, but now the sun appears to the west of the meridian, and of course keeps sinking rather than rising in the sky. Wait for sunset, and, ideally, watch it from the same spot that you occupied at sunrise. Mark the point on the horizon where sunset occurs, and estimate the position of this sunset point with respect to the due west point on the horizon. If you do this accurately (and here you should pause to consider how many generations of humans strove with vigor to achieve just this feat), you will find that the sunset point has an exact symmetry with the sunrise point that you recorded earlier in the day. If the sun rises at 18 degrees north of due east, it will set at 18 degrees north of due west. If sunrise occurs at 5 degrees south of east on the horizon, sunset will find the sun 5 degrees south of west. To our predecessors on Earth, this must have seemed a marvelous arrangement, a symmetry in the sky far more apparent, and far more perfect, than any seen on Earth. No wonder they ascribed to the heavens a nature entirely different from the world below! And yet the symmetry of sunrise and sunset provides just one piece of the beautifully symmetric sun cycle, the rhythm of the seasons that determines when to sow and when to reap. If you will take the time, you can see how the sun's changing traces across the sky fit into the cycles of spring, summer, winter, and fall, the eternal (by human standards) turns of the cosmic wheel that rule the Earth.

Activity Three:
The Cycles of the Year

Most of us have watched the sun rise and set without reflecting deeply on the astronomical implications of the sun's daily motion. To our ancestors, dependent on the sun, simply observing the sun set and rise was child's play, or, a bit more precisely, child's work. To adults, whose lives and fortunes depended on the cycle of the seasons, fell a much more difficult task: to track, remember, and predict the _changes_ in the places where the sun would rise and set. In any society numbering more than a few hundred, certain individuals became spiritual and cosmic mediators, persons seen as more intimately connected to the unearthly world above, typically rich in sky lore and therefore able to explain the puzzling phenomena of the heavens, often capable of predicting—sometimes correctly!—what would happen next in the skies. These priests or shamans understandably drew full respect from their tribe. You will now have an opportunity to try your hand at your own powers of observation and prediction. And you may console yourself by thinking of our poor climatologists, whose still impossible task it is to predict tomorrow's weather with certainty.

THE CHANGING POINTS OF SUNSET

Now that you have found a good spot to watch the sun go down, find the opportunity to watch the sun set on four or five days within a three-week interval, and record the points on the horizon where sunset occurs by making a simple sketch of the scene to the west. You may, of course, find that on some days clouds block your view of the sun as it slips below the horizon. If you persist, however, you will soon have a visual record of sunsets that clearly reveals the changes in the sun's location along your western horizon as it sets. If you are truly inspired, you can observe the points of sunrise as well as those of sunset. These sunrise observations should reveal exactly the same direction of motion, in precisely the same amounts of angular distance along the horizon, that you see for the points of sunset. I urge you, as you persevere in this task, to enjoy each sunrise and sunset and to observe not only their beauty but also the sense of peace and connectedness that you may experience from linking your daily routine to the sun's crossings of the horizon line. What will your record of sunsets (and possibly sunrises) show? Except for two special times of the year, your observations will soon reveal an unmistakable trend:

although the sun generally sets toward the west, your careful sketches of each day's sunsets will show *either that the sun has set farther to the north at each successive sunset, or that your sunsets have occurred progressively farther to the south.* In other words, you will discover that at any time throughout the year, the sunset position is moving in one of two possible directions, toward the north or toward the south. The same holds true for sunrise, whose position and movement always mirror that of sunset.

WHEN THE SUN STANDS STILL

The two exceptions to this rule describing how the sun sets and rises appear at the far northern and far southern points of sunset and sunrise. At the beginnings of winter and summer, the positions that the sun occupies on the horizon as it sets and rises seem to stand still for a few days. These are the winter and summer "solstices," whose Latin name means "sun still."

To our ancestors, the yearly "excursions" of the sunset and sunrise points along the horizon drew the attention they deserved, which was enormous. Each latitude north and south of the equator has its own precise values not

THE WANDERING SUN

The winter solstice, on December 21 or 22, and the summer solstice, on June 20 or 21, mark the times when the sunset and sunrise positions deviate the most from their average, intermediate locations. What are those average positions? Quite appropriately, the average sunset occurs exactly to the west, and the average sunset exactly to the east. Remember, though, that "average" means what it says. *Only* on the two equinox days do sunsets and sunrises actually occur at their average locations. The spring equinox, on March 20 or 21, and the fall equinox, on September 21 or 22, are the only days of the year when the sun rises directly in the east and sets exactly in the west.

How far to the north and south of these average positions does the sun rise and set? Here the wandering meets the wondering, because the horizon locations of sunset and sunrise on the solstice days depend on your latitude, that is, on how far north or south of the equator you happen to be. Those who live on the equator see the least deviation, though significant wandering still appears: the sunset and sunrise points at the solstices lie 23.5 degrees north and south of the points directly east and west. As you move farther from the equator, the sunset and sunrise points wander considerably more during the course of a year. At 40 degrees north of the equator, the latitude of Philadelphia, Denver, and Salt Lake City, sunsets and sunrises occur at a maximum deviation of 31 degrees to the north and south. At 45 degrees from the equator, typical of southern Germany, northern France, Boston, and Portland, Oregon, the maximum deviations are nearly 35 degrees. At 51 degrees, the latitude of southern England, the maximum excursions nearly reach 40 degrees. Still farther from the equator, at the latitude (55.5 degrees north) of Copenhagen and Glasgow, the sun's maximum excursion equals 45 degrees, meaning that on the day of the summer solstice, the sun rises halfway between the due east and due north points on the horizon, and sets halfway between the due west and due north points. Half a year later, on the winter solstice, the sun will rise halfway between due east and due south, and will set halfway between the due west and due south points of the compass. In those locations, the full swing between the farthest north and farthest south of the sun's rising and setting points equals 90 degrees, one-quarter of a full circle around the horizon.

only for the maximum sunset and sunrise excursions to the north and south that occur on the solstices, but also for the sun's position on the horizon as it rises or sets on every day of the year. The sole exception occurs on the equinoxes, when all observers see the sun rise directly in the east and set directly in the west. Every community, therefore, had to discover and to record its own pattern of the changes in the sun's position at sunset and sunrise. Many of them did so with a social energy that seems fantastic. Throughout the British Isles and northwestern France, for example, societies of past millennia erected rows or rings of large stones that marked out the sun's changing positions on the horizon. The best-known example, the concentric rings called Stonehenge, consists mainly of huge blocks of stone, each weighing many tons, that had to be dragged for dozens of miles from the sites where they could be quarried, then set into "trilithons," with one heavy stone resting high upon two others. A person standing in the center of Stonehenge's circles on the morning of the summer solstice will see the sun rise over the strategically placed "heel stone" about one hundred yards to the northeast. Other orientations of the circles of stone, and of other stones outside them, align with the sun's rising and setting positions on other key days of the year. By showing where the sun

rises and sets, Stonehenge enshrines for the ages what your sketch recorded for a couple of weeks. Astronomers interested in archaeology have found many similar devices around the world. In Mesoamerica, Peru, Egypt, southern Africa, and India, structures with ages measured in many centuries or even millennia still remain, often in highly dilapidated form, in their original alignments toward the sun's maximum excursions at rising and setting.

The great stone trilithons at Stonehenge once formed a complete circle. A person standing at the center of this circle on the day of the summer solstice would see the sun rise over a "heel stone" in the distance.

LONGER SUN PATHS IMPLY LONGER DAYS

Why did our ancestors take such care and expend such enormous effort in recording, and presumably in predicting, the points where the sun would rise and set? They did so because they saw, as you can still see, that these points are intimately connected with the paths that the sun takes across the sky. No matter where you are on Earth, you will see that the sun reaches its highest point in the sky as it crosses your meridian, the imaginary line joining the due north and due south points on any observer's horizon that passes through the overhead point, or zenith. Because the sun's risings and settings always occur symmetrically with respect to the meridian, every day of the year sees just as much time elapse between sunrise and local noon as between local noon and sunset.

A great difference occurs, however, in the *total* number of daylight hours on different days of the year. For northern-hemisphere observers, the farther the sun rises and sets to the north, the longer it will remain above the horizon, because it has a longer path to follow up to and over the meridian. Since the sun moves across the sky at a constant rate (more accurately, since the Earth spins at a constant rate), a longer path for the sun to follow implies a greater amount of time for the sun's motion to occur. Southern-hemisphere observers see the symmetrically reversed effect: for them, the farther to the *south* the sun rises and sets, the longer will be the path of

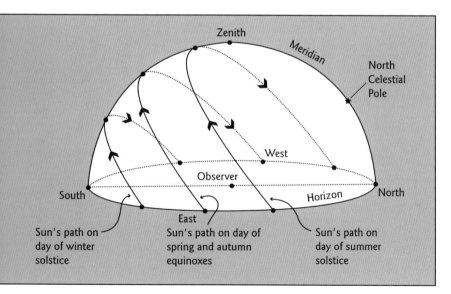

In the northern hemisphere on days close to the summer solstice, the sun will rise and set much farther to the north, and will remains much longer above the horizon, than it will near the day of the winter solstice.

the sun's journey across the sky, and the longer that journey will take.

SAFE MEASUREMENT OF THE SUN'S ALTITUDE

Here is one of life's problems you may not have confronted: how can you observe the sun's maximum height above the horizon at the time it crosses the meridian, while continuing to ensure the safety of your eyes by avoiding any direct gaze at the sun? Even our ancestors, hardy though they were, must have been sufficiently wise not to look for long at our life-giving star. By quick, averted glances, they could determine when the sun lay directly to the south, because they had long since determined the landmarks that would specify this compass point. (To achieve this goal, you can watch the stars at night, with no danger to your eyes at all: they too reach their maximum altitudes as they pass directly above the south point of your horizon.) Another method, the most appropriate in daylight, consists of watching your shadow and determining when it has grown shortest, a sign that the sun has reached its maximum altitude in the sky.

The best way to make this determination relies on the assistance of a friend (or the kindness of a stranger) who will measure your shadow's length while you admire it, avoiding, as always, any direct look at the sun. If your shadow's height exactly equals your own, the sun must have an altitude of 45 degrees, meaning that it stands halfway up from the horizon to the zenith. If your shadow is longer than you are tall, the sun has an altitude less than 45 degrees; if it is shorter than you, the sun must be more than 45 degrees above the horizon. This rule holds true, of course, for any object that stands vertically and casts a shadow. In Arthur Conan Doyle's story "The Musgrave Ritual," the great detective Sherlock Holmes uses this method to determine the length of the shadow that a long-vanished tree must have cast in marking the hiding spot of the lost crown of England. The shadow game reveals the sun's altitude perfectly well whenever the sun casts a shadow, not only when it crosses your meridian. To use this method, you will find useful the following numbers, which show how the length of your shadow, expressed in terms of your height, increases as the sun's altitude decreases:

LENGTH OF YOUR SHADOW (IN TERMS OF YOUR HEIGHT)	ALTITUDE OF SUN IN SKY (IN DEGREES)
0.1	84
0.2	79
0.3	73
0.4	68
0.5	63.5
0.6	59
0.7	55
0.8	51
0.9	48
1.0	45
1.1	42
1.2	40
1.3	37.5
1.4	35.5
1.5	34
1.6	32
1.7	30.5
1.8	29
1.9	28

LENGTH OF YOUR SHADOW (IN TERMS OF YOUR HEIGHT)	ALTITUDE OF SUN IN SKY (IN DEGREES)
2.0	26.5
2.2	24.5
2.4	22.5
2.6	21
2.8	19.5
3.0	18.5
3.5	16
4.0	14
4.5	12.5
5.0	11
5.5	10
6.0	9.5
6.5	9
7.0	8
8.0	7
9.0	6.3
10.0	5.7
12.0	4.5

CHANGES IN THE SUN'S ALTITUDE

The sun's altitude as it crosses the meridian changes significantly during the course of a year, though most of us record these variations only unconsciously. In Chicago, for example, the sun rises to a maximum altitude of 48 degrees above the southern horizon on the days of the equinoxes, but it reaches 71.5 degrees on the summer solstice and only 24.5 degrees on the winter solstice. You cannot fail to notice the difference between daytime's total light and the warmth of your days as the sun reaches nearly 80 percent of the zenith's altitude on the former date, but achieves only a pale 28 percent of the distance from horizon to zenith on the winter solstice. These changes in the sun's meridian altitude accompany what we notice more directly, the large differences between the numbers of daylight hours in summer and winter. As the sun rises farther to the south of east, achieves a much lower meridian altitude, and sets farther to the south of west, we receive less heat and light during the course of a day, and rightly call the season winter. Summer reverses the picture, with the sun achieving its maximum meridian altitude and making its greatest excursions to the north in its rising and setting.

As you move farther from the equator, these seasonal differences grow progressively larger as the sun's maximum excursions in rising and setting increase. Even though the difference between the sun's summer and winter meridian altitudes above the southern horizon remains constant at 47 degrees, the difference in the total amount of time that the sun remains above the horizon in summer and winter grows ever larger as you travel farther toward the pole. Finally, when you reach a latitude of 66.5 degrees, you encounter a situation in which the sun never sets on the day of the summer solstice, and never rises on the day of the winter solstice! Here, at the Arctic Circle, or at the Antarctic Circle in southern latitudes, you will meet the phenomenon of the "midnight sun," if you are fortunate to enjoy the day of summer solstice in northern Scandinavia or central Alaska. On that day and at that latitude, the sun will rise 47 degrees above the southern horizon and will then just fail to set at an altitude of 0 degrees at the point directly to your north. Less renowned, because it is far more depressing, comes the day of reckoning six months later, when "noontime dark" (or "noontime dusk," to be more accurate) describes the sun's failure to crest the horizon at any time during the day.

If you find yourself at the North or South Pole, as researchers now do, you can enjoy the perfect symmetry of seeing the sun circle the sky at a constant altitude. On the day of the lit solstice, the sun makes a tour around the sky at an altitude of 23.5 degrees;

on the dark one, six months later, the sun never comes within 23.5 degrees of rising! Halfway in between, on the days of the equinoxes, the sun skims

The shimmering curtains of the aurora arise when fast-moving electrically charged particles from the sun, guided by the Earth's magnetic field, collide with atoms dozens of miles above the Earth's surface.

all the way around the horizon at each of the poles, caught in its transition between six months above and six months below the horizon.

Most of us will never see the sun from the North or South Pole, where it maintains a constant altitude as it circles the sky. We can, however, travel with relative ease to the Arctic Circle to experience either a day when the sun never sets or (far less appealing, but airfares are lower then) never rises. Even in cities such as Oslo, Stockholm, and St. Petersburg, the summer solstice days have no real darkness, because even though the sun does set, it never sinks so far below the horizon that twilight turns to dusk. These "white nights" compensate for nearly "black days" half a year earlier.

THE AURORA

In addition to extremely long summer days and winter nights, those who live much closer to one of the Earth's poles than the majority of us enjoy an opportunity to savor a phenomenon rarely seen in the lower forty-eight United States: the aurora, a nighttime shimmer of light that arises as our atmosphere performs yet another protective function. The air above us not only screens out harmful ultraviolet rays from the sun but also defends us against streams of charged particles, shot from the sun's surface at speeds of hundreds of miles per second during outbursts called "solar storms." Unlike sunlight, which leaps the 93 million miles from the sun to the Earth in about eight minutes, these charged particles take a few days to arrive. When they do, they encounter the Earth's magnetic field, which funnels most of them into trajectories that encounter the atmosphere high above the Arctic and Antarctic regions. Molecules of oxygen and nitrogen then block these fast-moving particles, whose impacts make the molecules glow with an eerie light. Dozens of miles above the Earth, shimmering veils of red, green, and bluish light appear and pulsate, bestowing upon those below a fluttering veil of light, called the aurora borealis or aurora australis in its northern and southern appearances, respectively.

On rare occasions, auroral displays appear as far south as the mid–United States; should you hear, one night, of an aurora in your neck of the woods (city lights almost always overcome these lovely sheets of atmospheric glow), seize the opportunity to have a look, for it may not come again to that spot during your lifetime. In Japan, auroral displays command such great respect that many Japanese will travel far to see one. This fact helps support the winter tourist trade in Alaska and Norway, where the winter skies are dark almost around the clock and an aurora may appear at any moment, because the sun continuously emits some rapidly moving charged particles, although a solar storm raises this output many times over.

For the rest of us, without much expectation of a spectacular aurora, the nights of summer still yield to darkness, and winter days continue to bring us many hours of sunlight, as the sun sets and rises along its seemingly eternal cycle of motion. May we enjoy many more of these risings and settings, drinking them in all the more deeply now that we have experienced the pleasure to be gained from following the sun in its course through the sky.

MEDITATION

The simple exercise of watching the sun rise and set, and of noting how high it rises above the southern horizon, leads straightaway to the observations we have outlined, that the sun's points of rising and setting are symmetrical with respect to east and west, that they vary throughout the year in a cyclical manner, and that the sun's maximum altitude likewise follows the rhythm of the seasons. Indeed, these changes explain the seasons: we have warmer and longer days in summertime because the sun follows a longer track from rising to setting and rises higher above the southern horizon.

Early generations of humans reached a peak achievement by learning the sun's seasonal trajectories through the sky. Because humans are an inquisitive species, however, some people have always asked, *Why* does the sun follow different paths across the sky on different days of the year? In this chapter, I have deliberately concentrated on what you can see in the sky, and have not asked you to reflect on the celestial geometry that explains these phenomena. Take a moment now to ask yourself, How much of this was I taught in school? How much of it stuck in my brain?

We all learned that the sun, moon, and stars rise and set not because the sky turns around us, but rather because the Earth rotates once each day. Counterintuitive though this fact may be, we have come to remember and to accept it, so that I have not hesitated to mention the Earth's rotation as the true cause of the sun's daily motion across the sky. When it comes to the seasons, however, most of us have forgotten what we once knew. More precisely, in our intuitive hearts we never accepted the explanation as valid. Astronomers who seek to explain basic facts about the Earth often refer to a famous short film made at Harvard University, named "A Separate Universe." In this film, intelligent high-school and college students are asked to explain the cause of the seasons on Earth. Even though the film shows many of these students learning the true explanation, we see that they cannot retain it: when pressed, they revert to their intuition, which insists that the seasons change because the Earth changes its distance from the sun.

This explanation makes perfectly good sense—if it were true. The Earth does change its distance from the sun, and it receives less of the sun's light and heat when it has a distance greater than average. However, these changes in Earth-sun distance amount to no more than plus or minus 1.7 percent of the average distance, far too small to produce such significant effects as the seasons on Earth. The change-in-distance explanation proves to be a red herring, true but irrelevant. Note that if this were the true cause of the seasons, we would have summer or winter at the same time all over the Earth, rather than the actual seasonal changes, which simultaneously bring summer to the northern hemisphere and winter to the southern.

The true explanation of the seasons lies in the different paths that the sun takes through the sky, which are intimately connected with the changing locations of the sunrise and sunset points. I have found that people have no difficulty in accepting this explanation, because once again it corresponds to intuition, and indeed to intuition reinforced by experience for those who have taken the trouble to note how the sun crosses the sky. The difficulty arises when we are asked to make a complete change in our mental framework, to step (mentally!) off the Earth and to look at our planet as it orbits the sun. If we do so, we see how the sun's rays shine more directly on one hemisphere, less directly on the other, at the times of the solstices. Because the Earth's rotation axis tilts by 23.5 degrees from being perpendicular to the plane of the Earth's orbit, and because this axis always

points to the same direction in space, six months later we find the sun shining more directly on the once wintry hemisphere, less directly on the hemisphere where summer reigned half a year earlier.

To an astronomer, this mental picture encapsulates, on a global scale, what any observer will record from the Earth's surface. The mental model of a tilted, rotating Earth allows astronomers to calculate, as I have done, the maximum excursions of the sun's rising and setting points on the horizon, and the sun's maximum and minimum meridian altitudes, for any location on Earth. I have come to realize, however, that for most of us, experience and intuition rule. We all want answers, of course, but those that violate our intuitive feelings, which were formed long before we learned how to discriminate among competing explanations, can only rarely find complete acceptance in our hearts.

Scientists have confronted this conundrum and have mastered it, happily accepting the fact—often, indeed, reveling in it—that the truth about nature often contradicts intuition. Because our intuition arises from a highly limited set of experiences, confined to Earth and to a certain scale of distances, we can expect that the facts that we discover about domains other than our immediate surroundings almost certainly will violate our intuitive feelings. An essential point about science, not everyone's cup of tea, is that the truth is likely to be extraordinary in all senses of the word. (Do not confuse this with the notion that the extraordinary is likely to be true, the cornerstone of pseudoscientific approaches to reality.) When I say "truth," I mean, of course, the truth as scientists find it through the organized skepticism that they apply to the universe around them. Other ways exist to view the world, and no one can win the metaphysical argument that one approach provides a deeper truth than another. Greater usefulness, yes; greater appeal, certainly; but not greater truth, which remains a matter of individual judgment.

If you have enjoyed watching the sun, I invite you to take equal pleasure in the moon, the planets, and the stars. Each of them has stories to tell, but even more directly, each of them has its dance of light and dark, opening an avenue into a zone of wonder and understanding. Now that you have done the sun, come wander with me through the once fearsome, now human-friendly skies of the night.

Chapter *Two*

The Rabbit in the Moon

This photograph, taken from the Space Shuttle, shows the full moon as it rises above the Earth.

Everyone knows the moon, the light of the night sky, the only celestial object whose surface we can safely admire, for the sun shines far too brightly, and the planets and stars are far too distant for our detailed examination. Seen in bygone days as a pristine object of cosmic beauty, our moon still hangs in the heavens, but now, instead of offering a completely different kind of object, beckons us to visit another world, a solid globe fundamentally similar to Earth, though without our planet's water, air, and flourishing life.

Ancient observers of the sky saw a fitting and lovely duality in the sun and the moon, with the former shining by day and the other, at least at its brightest, illuminating the night. Some texts, in fact, find the moon more useful than the sun, since the moon shines at night, when it is needed most! Almost all past cultures, dominated by male thinkers, have seen a contrast between the male sun, whose strength appears in his great luminosity, and the much paler female moon, whose light plays a secondary role in the skies.

Whenever you take a good look at the moon, which you can do in safety (except through a telescope) because the moon shines with only one one-millionth of the sun's brightness, you will be struck by the brilliance of its apparently whitish surface, dotted with darker patches. The moon's whiteness reminds us of substances such as white paint, which reflect a high percentage of the incident sunlight. In actuality, however, the moon's brightness arises from the contrast between its light and the dark sky. We now know that the moon's surface is as dark as the ace of spades or an asphalt highway: only about 7 percent of the light that reaches the moon bounces back into space. If our satellite reflected light as well as the planet Venus does, it would shine ten times more brightly in our skies!

Even with its 7-percent solution to the question of light reflection, the moon does a fine job of lighting the night skies. To master lunar lore and the moon's motions, begin with a basic activity that you may find you have neglected for too long: find the rabbit in the moon.

Activity One:
See the Rabbit in the Moon

Look at the full moon; what do you see? For those of us reared in western European traditions, the man in the moon beams brightly upon you, with his broad, asymmetric face seeming to smile on Earth, more with his eyes than with his tilted mouth. Once you have been raised to see the man in the moon, your imprinted brain will stubbornly resist other ways to interpret the lunar markings. Give it a try, though, and test whether you can see what a majority of the world's population sees: the rabbit in the moon.

How can a human face turn into a rabbit? Much depends on whether you insist on perceiving the moon's darker features as a human face, or whether you focus more attention on the large "tears" seemingly wept by the left and smaller eye of "the man on the moon," which form the head and the two long ears of the rabbit. The rabbit's body consists of this man's eyes plus the dark splotches below the right eye. If you can't see it, don't fret; use the experience to reflect on the difficulty of revising a previously formed mind-set. If you have friends of Asian origin, ask them what they see in the moon. They will likely tell you that they always see a rabbit, and only with considerable effort can imagine a human face. Take a stroll in the moonlight with such a friend, and let each of you try to convince the other whether the rabbit or the face jumps out more quickly from the lunar surface.

If you cannot agree, or if you refuse to see either a man or a rabbit in the broad features of the moon's surface, you can try for a third alternative, the toad in the moon. The toad's head appears in the bright features of the moon that seem to protrude upward from the lower edge, forcing their way into what we would call the center of the face of the man in the moon. An ethnological survey of lunar tradition would show that different cultures have seen a rabbit, a toad, or a man's face, but that the dominant mental projection has been the rabbit in the moon, seen by nearly all the inhabitants of southern and eastern Asia; as well as the Mayas, Aztecs, and native Americans of the southwestern United States; and the Saxons of northern Europe. Although the man in the moon has appeared in thousands of cartoons, he played little or no role in the mythology of ancient Greece or Rome. In contrast, the fecundity of rabbits has led naturally to the association of the moon with fertility in the cultures with a rabbit regard for the moon. Even today, Chinese families around the world gather to celebrate the midsummer moon festival, which includes special mooncakes, sold in boxes that often show the moon goddess, Heng O, carrying a rabbit as a symbol of good fortune.

WHY DON'T WE SEE BOTH SIDES OF THE MOON?

If you look carefully at the moon over a few days' time, and search your memory for earlier views of the moon, you will be struck by a singular fact: we always see the same face, the same rabbit, or the same toad. How can this be so? If the moon is a round, rotating object similar to the Earth, why don't we see all the way around it as it turns?

The moon's one-faced appearance drew little attention in cultures that regarded celestial objects as entirely unlike our Earth. From their perspective, the moon might well be a flat disk skimming across the sky, but never a spherical object, similar in shape and composition to our Earth, though only one-quarter as wide. Once we perceive that the moon is a solid, round object, however, its single-faced appearance demands an explanation, and we must conclude that the moon has only one way to keep the same face always pointed toward Earth. As the moon moves around us, it must rotate at just the rate required to keep one side pointed toward the Earth and the other side hidden. In other words, the moon spins on its axis once each month, in exactly the same amount of time that it takes to move once around the Earth.

Our intuition, however, insists that the statements above make no sense at all. Surely, intuition says, if the moon keeps the same face pointed toward the Earth, this must imply that the moon does not rotate at all! But a moment's thought can overcome intuition. If the moon did not rotate, then by definition the face with the rabbit would always point toward the same direction in space. In that case, as the moon moved around the Earth, it would show each of its sides to us, like a square-dance partner doing a do-si-do around you. In contrast, a dance partner who keeps his gaze fixed upon you will see all four walls of the room behind you as he circles your spot

On the moon, "Earthrise" occurs when the Earth appears above the horizon.

on the floor. Similarly, either side of the moon must be directed toward all the points of a circle as the moon moves around the Earth with its rabbit side always facing us.

I have taken this excursion from what we see in the sky deliberately, in order to remind you that once we suspend the view that heaven has its own rules, even such straightforward observations as the fact that we always see the rabbit face of the moon can provoke deep thought, worthy of more than a moment's reflection. Some people find this the best part of astronomy, while others have little use for it. In this book, we are more concerned with what we see than with what we know, but on occasion it helps to remember that what we see may be simultaneously amazing and misleading.

THE MOON ILLUSION

One of the most striking aspects of the moon's appearance resonates in our brains without actually occurring in nature. As the full moon clears the eastern horizon, it appears to hang in the evening sky, a great bright globe that often seems larger to you than your memory of the daytime sun. A few hours later, when the moon has climbed higher in the sky, it still shines brightly and continues to show you its rabbit face, but if you ask one hundred people, "When does the full moon appear largest to you?" one hundred of them will answer, "When the moon has just risen."

How can this be so? Technically, the moon seen near the horizon cannot be closer to Earth than the moon seen high in the sky; indeed, the moon on the horizon is actually a bit farther away. Why, then, does the "moon illusion," as astronomers call it, work such powerful magic? Could our atmosphere somehow refract moonlight in special ways when we see the moon near the horizon? No, it turns out that this cannot explain what we see. Could the moon somehow be brighter, and therefore impress our eyes the more, soon after it rises? No, the moon actually shines more brightly when high in the sky. Photographs taken of the moon at different locations in the sky do not show a size difference—demonstrating that the apparent difference in sizes arises entirely in our brains: we *see* the moon as larger when it is near the horizon. While the reason that we do so is not yet fully understood, we do know that because we spend most of our time gazing in directions roughly parallel to the horizon, and relatively little looking more or less straight up, our perceptions change as we lose the visual cues close to the horizon. To check this out, pick a time when the rising moon seems particularly large and looming, face away from the moon, bend over, and look at the moon through your legs. (May you have youthful bendability through all your long life!) You will perceive, I predict, that the moon then looks not so large as before.

THE MOON'S MOTION AGAINST THE STARRY BACKGROUND

Once you have returned to an upright posture, try to find a bright star or two close to the moon that will allow you to record the moon's position with respect to the stars. If you are devoted to astronomy, draw a simple sketch of the moon and stars nearby; then, when you return to look at the moon an hour or two later, you will find that it has moved visibly with respect to your starry markers. In fact, in every hour the moon will move through an angular distance of half a degree, equal to the moon's apparent diameter on the sky. And in what direction does the moon move? Take a good look, repeat the procedure on successive nights to be sure of your result, and you will find that the moon keeps "slipping" backwards with respect to the stars. As the sky seems to turn, carrying the stars and the moon itself toward the west, the moon moves modestly in the opposite direction, toward the east, in the direction backward to the overall wheeling of the heavens. As a result, the moon remains above the horizon about half an hour longer than it would if this slippage did not take place.

If you find the moon in the sky on a particular night, will it be in the same place on the next night at the same time? Close, but not exactly. Because the moon slides steadily in an eastward direction, it will rise about 50 minutes later on each successive day or night. Try finding the moon as it rises on one night (this works especially well close to the time of a full moon) and note the moment when you observe the moon closest to the eastern horizon, which will be the first time that you see it on that night. If you look for the moon the next evening at the same.time, you are likely to find that the moon has not yet risen, and that you must wait through part of an hour for the moon to crest the horizon. While the average daily slippage equals 50 minutes, the actual amount varies depending on the season of the year and the latitude at which you make your observations, so that you may find an interval somewhere between 45 and 55 minutes.

Activity Two:
The Phases of the Moon

Once you have deepened your acquaintance with the moon's appearance, you are ready to embark on a fundamental activity that fascinated bygone generations—watching the phases of the moon. Many of your friends labor under the delusion that the moon passes from quarter moon to full moon, or even changes from a crescent into a full moon, during a single night. None of your great-grandparents would have been so completely out of touch with celestial reality as this, so I urge you to redress the ills of modern society and to savor the changing phases of the moon.

To enjoy the cycle of the moon's phases to the fullest, you should pick a point in that cycle and then follow the moon through its next complete cycle, which lasts approximately one month, or, as the Anglo-Saxons spelled it, one "moonth." The intimate connection between the phases of the moon and the heights of the tides causes almost every newspaper to announce these phases, often in its weather section or in the sporting section for boating enthusiasts. If your newspaper doesn't fit into this category, or if you choose not to plan so far ahead, fall back on the old-fashioned approach: wait until you can see the moon in the sky on a particular night, and start your observational cycle from that date. You must, of course, anticipate that cloudiness will cause you to miss one or more days in the full cycle, but with a reasonably good memory you can reconstruct what must have occurred on the nights that you missed seeing the moon, just as our ancestors did.

Most societies that marked the progression of day by following the phases of the moon have recorded each cycle as beginning with the slim crescent moon, which the Islamic calendar still uses to mark the beginning of each month. We can make things easier by starting with the most glorious phase of the moon, the full moon. At full moon, the moon rises at sunset and sets at sunrise, so you can follow the moon until dawn if you wish, watching it sink below the western horizon as the sun rises in the east.

FOLLOWING THE FULL MOON ACROSS THE SKY

If you plan to follow the full moon as it crosses the sky, you must be prepared to engage yourself from sunset to sunrise, the times that correspond to moonrise and moonset, because the full moon always appears on the sky in the direction nearly opposite the sun. If you perform this activity, you will find that the moon's path, like the sun's, exhibits a splendid symmetry between its going up and its coming down. The full moon takes just as long to travel from moonrise to its highest point in the sky, at a time close to midnight, as it does to pass from that high mark down to its setting. Like the sun's, the moon's high point in the sky occurs as it crosses the meridian, standing high above the south point on the horizon.

What altitude does the full moon reach as it crosses the meridian? Intriguingly, the full moon rises much higher in winter than in summer. This makes good sense once you realize that the full moon lies almost directly opposite the sun on the sky. Full moon occurs when we see the moon's entire lit half, so the moon must then be on the opposite side of the Earth from the sun. Because the sun takes a year to circle the sky, moving slowly against the background of stars (see chapter 7), the full moon occupies essentially the same position on the sky that the sun did six months earlier, and will reach once again in another six months. If you follow the sun through the course of a year, you will see that summer and winter differ in the amount of time that the sun remains above the horizon and the maximum altitude that the sun reaches at its meridian crossing. So too with the moon, but the full moon's position corresponds to the sun's half a year before or afterward.

If our seasons depended on moonlight rather than sunlight, they would be exactly reversed, since the moon rises highest in the sky during winter and least above the southern horizon during summer. How fortunate for us on Earth that we receive the maximum light from the full moon during the longest, coldest, nights of winter, when the moon crosses the sky along a track reminiscent of the sun in summer! How easily we can spare some of the full moon's light in summer, when the moon's trajectory across the sky closely corresponds to the sun's winter motion!

Nature could hardly have done better with her full moon, but in fact she has. Because of the different paths that the moon can take across the sky, the full moon close to the fall equinox seems to last longer. More precisely, the time interval between moonrises on successive days, which averages 50 minutes but can be shorter or longer, reaches a minimum as fall begins. This means that the evenings just before and just after the full moon in September and October are more full moon–like than they are on the other days of the year that likewise fall close to the day of full moon. In olden times, this phenomenon, called the "harvest moon," helped farmers as they labored into the night to gather their crops.

After full moon, the moon "wanes," losing a bit more of its former fullness every night. The first night after full moon may show no visible difference, but the next few days make this fact obvious. Be prepared, however, to stay up sufficiently late to observe the moon's appearance! Since the moon rises about 50 minutes later on each successive night, five or six nights after full moon will find you waiting nearly until midnight for the moon to rise. Almost seven and a half days after full moon, the moon reaches the phase of "last quarter." At this time, the moon appears half lit and half dark. We call this a "quarter" rather than a "half" moon because this phase quarters the month, marking the time when one-quarter of a month has elapsed after full moon. The last-quarter moon always rises close to local midnight, crosses the meridian near dawn, and sets at a time close to local noon. If you miss seeing the moon in its last-quarter phase because you called it a night before the moon rose, you can find it in the morning by looking toward the west and catching the moon as it prepares for its own down time.

As the moon continues to wane, it rises later and later, so its next phases, during which the half-lit moon diminishes to a thin crescent, find the moon rising long after midnight. Because the moon always stays above the horizon for about half a day, this means that the moon sets long after noon and remains above the horizon throughout most of the daytime. To observe this crescent, you must either rise before dawn to see the slimming moon in darkness, or look for the pale, thin crescent in the glare of the daylight. Since the ever-thinning lunar crescent shines with a decreasing brightness, finding the moon long after its last-quarter phase poses a problem. On each of the days between last quarter and new moon, the moon moves closer to the sun on the sky and becomes more difficult to observe. Finally, on the last day before new moon, the slender crescent sets in the west less than an hour before the sun does, extremely difficult to see.

At new moon, 14¾ days after full moon, the moon appears close to the sun on the sky as it passes almost directly between ourselves and the sun. At this time, you will not see the moon at all without special knowledge and equipment, because the dark side of the moon faces us, while its lit side faces away toward the sun, the light-giver of the solar system. Once we pass new moon, defined by the moon's closest approach to the sun on the sky, the moon again becomes visible in the early evening, setting in the west soon after the sun does. During the first few days after new moon, you can see the moon best soon after sunset, as a lovely glowing crescent, with the crescent's "horns" pointing away from the sun.

The nearly seven and a half days that pass between new moon and the lunar first quarter find the moon waxing (growing), which means that you will see the illuminated portion of the moon become larger on

The Tilt of the Moon's Orbit

If the moon's orbit around the Earth did not tilt slightly with respect to the plane of the Earth's orbit around the sun, each new moon would produce an eclipse of the sun, as the moon's motion carried it directly in front of our star. The 5-degree tilt of the moon's orbit with respect to the Earth's produces a near-miss at most new moons, with the moon passing either a bit below or a bit above the sun. Only about one new moon in 15 brings a total eclipse of the sun.

Earthshine

If you wait until dark, and find the crescent moon still above your horizon, you can look for "Earthshine" on the dark portion of the moon. A careful gaze under clear skies will prove that you can actually *see* the moon's dark side, rather than merely noting that darkness rules on that portion of the lunar surface because the sun shines only on the other half of the moon. How can the moon's dark side, blocked from sunlight by its lit half, provide any light to us? The dark side produces no light of its own, but it does reflect into space a fraction of the sunlight that bounces off the Earth, some of which happens to strike the moon. A small portion of this "Earthlight" reflected by the moon heads in our direction, so we can see the dark side with a modest effort,

thanks to our own planet's reflection of sunlight. A lovely old phrase describes the much darker, though still visible, remainder of the moon and the bright crescent around it as "the old moon in the new moon's arms."

While you enjoy the Earthshine on the moon, take a moment to notice a related phenomenon: the bright crescent appears larger than the dark remainder. This must be another moon illusion, since greater illumination can hardly increase the size of an object. Your eyes and your brain are indeed playing a trick on you, for they register a bright object as a bit larger than a dim object with the same angular size.

each successive night. As this happens, the moon sets later, as indeed it does on every successive day, and it also moves farther from the sun in the sky. A few days after new moon, you will find that the moon sets only after shining brightly for several hours after sunset in the night skies toward the west. At the moment of first- quarter moon, your lines of sight to the moon and sun form a right angle (90 degrees), so if you look at the sky a couple of hours before sunset, you can sense the sun well above the southwestern horizon, while the half-lit moon, 90 degrees away on the sky, rides high in the sky to the southeast. At the time of the first-quarter moon, the moon rises at noon, crosses the meridian close to sunset, and sets at midnight. During the nearly eight days following, as the moon waxes toward its full-moon phase, it rises later every night, showing more and more of its lit half to us, once more regaining its familiar and benign full-moon appearance.

Finally, 29.53 days after the previous full moon, the moon becomes full once again. Notice that although we can mark an exact moment when the moon is technically at its fullest (most directly opposite the sun on the sky), in real life we count by days, and look for the full moon either twenty-nine or thirty days after the previous one, when once again the moon rises just about at sunset, sets at sunrise, and shows us its entire lit hemisphere. At this moment, the moon's far side, always hidden from our view, coincides with its dark side, the side away from the sun. As you have seen, the moon's near and far sides never exchange their characters, so you always see the rabbit in the moon or the man in the moon, which mark the lunar near side. But

as the moon moves in its orbit, the sun shines successively on all parts of the moon, so the moon's lit and dark halves do exchange their locations; if they did not, we would never see the moon's phases.

TIDES AND THE MOON'S PHASES

In addition to providing a light in the night skies, the moon also plays the major role in raising the tides in Earth's oceans that help to support the hosts of creatures that depend on the tides' ebb and flow. These tides track the motions of the moon, with high tides occurring, roughly speaking, when the moon is either highest in the sky or lowest underfoot (that is, halfway in time between its highest risings). This coupling of the tides to the moon's position in the sky can easily be tracked, so it seems odd at first glance that almost no earlier societies saw the moon as crucial in raising them. Confusion about the tides, however, doubtless arose in large part from the appearance of *two* high tides and *two* low tides in every day—a fact that still causes perplexity in freshman astronomy classes.

Because the various parts of the Earth have different distances from the moon and the sun, they feel

SPRING TIDES AND NEAP TIDES

If we had no moon, the sun would raise tides in the oceans, but they would be only about one-third as large, and would therefore allow only much smaller regions of the ocean shores to participate in the tide-bound behavior that keeps tide pools burbling with biological activity. In reality, the moon and sun together produce the tides, with the moon in the lead role. When the sun and moon are nearly in a line with respect to the Earth, at the times of full moon or new moon, we find especially large "spring tides," when the ocean rises ("springs" in the old terminology) to noticeably greater heights at high tide. In contrast, when the sun and moon appear at nearly perpendicular directions as seen from Earth, we see the moon half lit and half dark as a first-quarter or last-quarter moon, and the tide-raising effects of the sun and moon oppose each other. Then we find much more modest "neap tides," whose name, akin to our familiar word "nap," implies that the tides are taking a rest. Since spring tides and neap tides alternate twice every time that the moon goes through its cycle of phases, we can easily see that some connection must exist between these two phenomena. Nevertheless, the fact that the moon, with help from the sun, raises the tides in the Earth's ocean remained a subject of mystery and debate until the late Renaissance, five centuries ago.

differing amounts of gravitational force from the moon and sun. The oceans react to these differences much more readily than the land does, slipping slightly back and forth with respect to the continents to produce the tides that we see on the sea shores. The details of this process tend to create high tides both when the moon is highest and when it is lowest.

THE CALENDAR: FITTING THE MOON'S CYCLE OF PHASES INTO A YEAR

The heavens have always furnished humanity with two fundamental and significant markings of time, the day and the year. We live by daily rhythms, while our agricultural activities—and thus all modern societies—depend on the seasons of the year. These two cycles arise from the Earth's rotation, which carries each part of our planet through day and night, and on the different paths that the sun takes across the sky, which are the result of our yearly motion around the sun. If we had no moon, these two time markers would have to suffice. In that case, our calendars would almost certainly divide the year into quarters, marked out by the four days of the equinoxes and the solstices. The summer and winter solstices, as we have seen, occur at the extreme points of the sun's motion, the days when the sun rises and sets as far north or as far south as it can, and makes either its longest or its shortest journey across the sky. Halfway between, the spring and fall equinoxes bring equal amounts of day and night to every part of the Earth, and mark the midpoint of the swing from one extreme to the other.

Until the eighteenth century, most of Europe and America used a calendar that began each new year on March 25, taken to represent the spring equinox. The names of the last four months of our year—September, October, November, and December—retain an echo of this era by telling us with their Latin roots that these were the seventh, eighth, ninth, and tenth months of the year.

In dividing the year, civilization now concentrates heavily on the month, and on its near-quartering, the week, which has no clear connection to celestial motions. The cycle of the moon's phases surely drew attention all over the world, not least because the moon's cycle of phases corresponds, closely though not perfectly, to the female menstrual cycle. It must have seemed entirely natural to record events on a

A SUN-BASED CALENDAR

To subdivide a calendar based only on the sun, we would probably cut each quarter of the year in two, and possibly cut once again, so a year would consist of eighths and possibly sixteenths. Two small remnants of this approach actually exist: Groundhog Day, on February 2, and Halloween, on October 31. These "cross-quarter days" derive from Celtic reckoning, which created "Imbolg" and "Samhain." Imbolg, now also called "Candlemas" (the day when Jesus was presented in the temple, forty days after his circumcision), lies halfway between the winter solstice and the spring equinox, whereas "Samhain," pronounced "sah-win" and meaning "summer's end," occurs halfway between the fall equinox and the winter solstice. The ancient Celts worried that these halfway times, which they used to mark the key points of the year, could snap the fabric of reality, loosing chaos on the world, or at least a host of demons. We still find this notion lurking in Halloween (the Eve[ning] preceding the day of all Hallows, meaning all Saints), which we celebrate on Samhain.

Had we no moon, we would go through the year Imbolging and Samhaining. Today, however, everyone notes the festivals of February 2 and October 31 without realizing their implications for the calendar, which include the "six more weeks of winter" (roughly the time from Groundhog Day to the spring equinox) that will occur, according to tradition, if the groundhog sees his own shadow on Imbolg. Halloween, not much more than five weeks after the fall equinox and more than seven weeks before the winter solstice, has a remarkably poor location for an accurate cross-quarter day, but has nevertheless been celebrated at the end of October for many centuries.

less-than-yearly time scale by employing the interval between one new moon and the next (or one full moon and the next), which equals 29.53 days. Those who kept track of the moon's phases soon saw that 29.5 days provides a remarkably accurate approximation to the lunar cycle. If you want to create a calendar based on the moon, therefore, you need months of 30 days, or, to produce far better accuracy, months that alternate between 29 and 30 days in length.

But a competing pressure existed, utterly irresistible in most societies: the year. By recording the recurrence of the seasons over a few centuries, well-established societies soon learned that a year lasts approximately 365 days, and more advanced ones came to the still more accurate figure of 365.25 days. (The actual interval from spring equinox to spring equinox equals 365.2422 days.) Since the sun, not the moon, drove the cycles of planting, growing, and harvesting, agricultural communities used a solar calendar with lunar subdivisions, just as we do today. Only one difficulty then lies in the way of calendrical satisfaction: you can't fit a whole number of lunar months into a year. This holds true whether you use 29 days, 29.5 days, or 30 days for the length of the moon's cycle of phases. Instead, what you find is that each year contains somewhat more than 12 full moon cycles. Twelve times 29.5 days equals 354 days, so in fact each year includes just about 12 lunar cycles plus 11.25 days, which equals 12.38 times one complete cycle of the moon's phases.

This ".38" has baffled calendar makers through the ages. Today, we might consider moving the moon into a different orbit, so that it would move a bit more slowly and 12 months would fit exactly into a year, but for our predecessors, the calendar issue could not be so easily resolved. Some societies, like the Romans, adopted months with 30 or 31 days (plus the oddity of February), so that 12 months would include a total of

365 days, leaving the lunar cycles to play second fiddle. We still use the Roman approach to the calendar, with February truncated because the Roman Emperor Caesar Augustus wanted the length of his month (August) to equal that of his predecessor Julius Caesar's (July), and took a day from a month already shortened for similar purposes. Julius Caesar gained his fame in the calendar world not so much by hogging a month's name but rather by introducing leap years, the one year in every four when February gains an extra day. This increases the length of the average year from 365 to 365.25 days. As a result, the "Julian calendar" seemed to work quite well, and passed into European civilization without objection. Because eleven of the months each contain 30 or 31 days, and because 29.53 days elapse between successive full moons, every few years brings us a "blue moon," the old name for a month in which two full moons happen to fall.

As time passed, however, the fact that the year reckoned by the calendar lasts a tiny bit longer than the actual time between successive spring equinoxes (365.2422 days) began to grow apparent. Every four centuries, the Julian calendar introduces three days more than the motions of the sun require. These extra days came to annoy those who followed the seasons carefully; Dante, in his *Paradiso,* spoke darkly of "the hundredth part which ye neglect," which would eventually cause spring to occur in January. In 1582, Pope Gregory corrected the Julian calendar, shortening it by three days in every four centuries with an edict that century years such as 1600, 1700, and 1800 would not be leap years unless they were evenly divisible by four hundred. The Gregorian calendar received immediate acceptance in Catholic countries and rejection in Protestant regions. Two centuries later, in 1751, England (and therefore the American colonies) swung over to the Gregorian calendar, dropping eleven days (as was then necessary) from that year and actually provoking some riots among those who felt cheated of time. This introduction of the Gregorian calendar, which was accompanied by setting the start of the new year at January 1 instead of March 22, means that dates such as George Washington's birthday must be treated carefully. Washington was born (so he felt) on February 11, 1731/2, but we celebrate his birthday on February 22, the date when it would have occurred if the Gregorian calendar had already been in use.

SOLAR YEARS AND LUNAR MONTHS

Must we abandon all hope of achieving a calendar that reconciles the solar year of 365.2422 days with the lunar month of 29.53 days? Sadly, the two cycles remain fundamentally incompatible, so each society must choose a calendar that gives priority to one of the two cycles. Attempts to somehow accommodate these two periods of time have often relied on what astronomers now call the Metonic cycle, which the Greek astronomer Meton apparently first noted during the fifth century B.C., although the cycle may have been known in China even earlier. Meton saw that 19 solar years almost exactly equal 235 lunar months in length. This means that every 19 years, the same phase of the moon will occur on the same day of the year, throughout the entire year. Because this coincidence is not exact, the rule holds true for a century or so and then requires adjustment, but it suggests a way to make things fit. If this strikes you as complex (and it ought to!), pause to consider that we step back several millennia into a time when the game was worth a host of candles.

We can make a workable calendar that accommodates both the sun and moon by taking months that are 29 and 30 days long. With six of each, we reach a year that is 354 days long, as we have seen, and would soon be far out of step with the seasons. We therefore add additional months to seven years out of every nineteen. Six of these "intercalary months" have 30 days each, and the seventh has 29 days. This brings the 19-year total of days to the proper amount for year that averages 365.25 days. The Jewish calendar works on the basis outlined above, with an extra month, called Ve'Adar (second Adar), added to seven years in every nineteen. Thus the Jewish calendar combines the sun and the moon, a mark of respect to both.

If you lived in the desert, where seasons have less importance than they do elsewhere, you might pay closer attention to the moon's phases than to the changing tracks of the sun across the sky. The Islamic calendar, which follows this guideline, sets the beginning and end of the year, as well as its festivals and holy days, by the cycle of lunar phases, and makes a year out of 12 cycles, equal to 354 days. As a result, Ramadan, the holiest Islamic month, always begins on the ninth month of the year, at the moment when the first crescent appears after new moon, and ends with the next new lunar crescent. Since this calendar worries not about the sun, Ramadan can occur in any season of the year, and more Islamic years have passed since Islam began (in what our calendar records as 622 A.D.) than we would count, because the Islamic year has 11 fewer days than ours. In contrast, the western calendar lets the moon run free and tracks only the sun. We do keep months of 28, 29, 30, or 31 days, but we make no adjustments that would keep the moon's phases in step with the calendar, as the Metonic cycle does.

The Gregorian calendar stays in step with the sun for many thousands of years, so we can wait a while before clamoring for a new attempt to fit the months into a year. Let us turn our attention to an equally complex, but far more impressive phenomenon involving the sun and moon, the eclipses they occasionally produce as they dance through the skies.

Activity Three:
Eclipses of the Moon and the Sun

Father sun and mother moon have their interactions, which first puzzled and then gladdened the lives of our forebears. One of the most evident facts about the sun and moon is that they both have the same size in the sky. Although the sun shines about a million times more brightly than the full moon, both objects produce their light from a disk half a degree across, so

that 720 suns or moons could sit shoulder to shoulder in a complete circle of 360 degrees around the horizon. You might reasonably conclude, if further facts were lacking, that the sun and moon appear to have the same angular size because they have the same diameter and the same distance from us. On the other hand, you might pause to reflect on a fact that our ancestors quickly recognized, that the moon moves far more quickly than the sun with respect to the starry background. This tends to imply that the moon must be closer to the Earth, and indeed most early pictures of the cosmos drew just this conclusion. In that case, the moon must have a smaller diameter than the sun does, or else its lesser distance would make it appear larger than the sun in our skies.

We now know that the sun lies fully four hundred times farther from us than the moon, so that in order to appear to us with the same angular size, the sun must be four hundred times wider than the moon. This is a cosmic coincidence of a high order, unknown elsewhere in the solar system or anywhere beyond the sun's family of planets. Other planets have moons, but their distances from each of those planets fail to have the near-perfect values that would give them an angular size nearly the same as the sun's when seen from that planet.

The luck of the cosmic draw has therefore created a situation in which the moon, if it happens to pass directly between ourselves and the sun, can just cover the entire disk of sunlight, producing that most marvelous of astronomical spectacles, a total solar eclipse. Solar eclipses threw the fear of the gods into our ancestors, even after they had mastered techniques not only of surviving but also of predicting these moments of darkness.

Just as the moon can come between ourselves and the sun to produce a solar eclipse, our planet can pass directly between the moon and the sun, creating an eclipse of the moon. Because observing a total solar eclipse during the next decade requires that you to plan far in advance for a long trip, possibly an expensive one to a site where the other tourists have booked all the good hotels, this activity calls for you only to observe a lunar eclipse. For this delight, you must still plan ahead, but you should be able to enjoy the spectacle without having to go farther than a site with a clear night sky.

The table on page 39 lists the total lunar eclipses that will be visible on Earth through the year 2010.

Note that the length of a total lunar eclipse can rise as high as an hour and a half. In addition, the geographical locations from which totality will be visible occupy much larger regions of the globe than they do for total eclipses of the sun, since they basically include the half of the Earth that happens to face the moon during the lunar eclipse.

In contrast to a total eclipse of the sun, during which the moon paints a thin ribbon of darkness over the Earth as it moves in its orbit, the entire moon becomes eclipsed when the bulk of our own planet, much larger than the moon, blocks sunlight from all of the lunar surface. The moon therefore nearly disappears when eclipsed. Indeed, if the Earth had no atmosphere, the moon would then vanish from sight completely. However, because the Earth's atmosphere acts like a lens and refracts sunlight, it bends some of the sun's rays onto the moon's surface, saving the eclipsed moon from total invisibility. As the Earth's atmosphere refracts sunlight, it bends more red light than violet light onto the moon. This causes the moon to turn dark red-brown during a total lunar eclipse. One of the most intriguing aspects of watching eclipses of the moon rests in the fact that each one gives the eclipsed moon a different shade of red, owing to the different atmospheric conditions then prevailing on Earth.

We have no way to know how red the moon looked in 1504, during Columbus's fourth voyage to the Americas, when the explorer and his companions felt themselves in danger from the inhabitants of Jamaica. Columbus then consulted an almanac he had providentially carried with him. (As the astronomer Edwin Krupp has noted, if he had landed in Mexico among the Maya, they would have had an equal or better almanac.) Finding that a total eclipse of the moon was

A total eclipse of the sun occurs when the moon passes directly between the Earth and the sun on a point along its slightly elliptical orbit sufficiently close to the Earth for the moon to cover the sun completely.

TOTAL ECLIPSES OF THE MOON THROUGH THE YEAR 2010

Date	Time of total eclipse	Regions where total eclipse can be seen
2003 May 16	53 min	central Pacific, the Americas, Europe, Africa
2003 November 9	24 min	the Americas, Europe, Africa, central Asia
2004 October 28	1 hour 21 min	the Americas, Europe, Africa, central Asia
2007 March 3	1 hour 14 min	the Americas, Europe, Africa, Asia
2007 August 28	1 hour 31 min	east Asia, Australia, Pacific, the Americas
2008 February 21	5 min 20 sec	central Pacific, the Americas, Europe, Africa
2010 December 21	1 hour 13 min	east Asia, Australia, Pacific, the Americas, Europe

due, Columbus informed the natives that the gods were angry and would therefore remove the moon for about an hour on a particular night; they should watch and take heed, generating and demonstrating better adulation of their visitors if they wanted the moon to survive. On the night fixed for the event, the reddish moon smiled on Columbus (whether he had a speech ready for a cloudy night has gone unrecorded). The natives indeed showed renewed respect, as your friends will do for you once you explain the basics of a lunar eclipse.

You might think that since a lunar eclipse plunges the entire moon into darkness, whereas a solar eclipse strongly affects only a tiny part of the Earth, people would pay more attention to eclipses of the moon than to those of the sun. However, solar eclipses receive far more attention because they deprive *us* of sunlight. Furthermore, a total eclipse of the sun occurs only rarely at any particular location, because the moon's shadow traces out only a thin ribbon of darkness as it passes over the Earth. On average, any terrestrial location will see a total solar eclipse about once every three centuries. For societies without a long folk memory, each total eclipse of the sun must have come as a com-

plete shock, made even more fearful by the fact that many partial eclipses would have come and gone without the moon completely covering the sun, thus generating a false sense of confidence. Total solar eclipses could have played an important role in history, intervening at crucial moments to impress those beneath the moon's shadow with the need to pay more attention to the sky gods. One instance does exist in the historical record, some two and a half millennia ago, when a full-scale battle stopped in mid-fight as a total eclipse of the sun shocked the participants, reminding them, perhaps, that their activities were not the surest path to happiness. Since then, however, thousands of total solar eclipses have been visible somewhere on Earth without much lasting impact on the mad behavior of crowds or the calm authority of kings.

The table below, which lists the total eclipses of the sun that will occur through the year 2010, includes especially long-duration ones in 2009 and 2010. Quite typically, these eclipses will occur in faraway lands, so if you have a desire to go to China, for example, the end of the decade could be your moment.

Although these eclipse situations are fundamentally symmetrical as seen by a cosmic outsider, from our

Earthly perspective they differ radically in both their appearance and their symbolic implications. A solar eclipse cuts off light from a thin swath of the Earth's surface, the part of the Earth that lies within the moon's shadow. Racing along its orbit, the moon casts that shadow, only eighty miles across in an average eclipse, along several thousand miles of the Earth's surface. Thus, only one part in ten thousand of the Earth's surface undergoes the darkness of a total solar eclipse, while the rest of the Earth experiences either no eclipse or merely the partial phases, in which the moon covers only a portion of the sun's disk.

However, even an eclipse that covers 99 percent of the sun's disk, allowing only 1 percent to deliver sunlight, will leave the sun shining as brightly as it does on an overcast day. Partial solar eclipses therefore attract little attention today, although many of our ancestors were baffled when they saw part of the sun disappear, an event that they often interpreted as a fearsome distension of the sun's usual shape. Today, only a total solar eclipse makes much of an impression. Since this can occur only in a highly limited portion of Earth, only a tiny fraction of the population can be startled and amazed by any particular eclipse.

TOTAL ECLIPSES OF THE SUN THROUGH THE YEAR 2010

Date	Time of total eclipse	Regions where total eclipse can be seen
2002 December 4	2 min 4 sec	southern Africa, Indonesia, Australia
2003 November 23	1 min 57 sec	Australia, New Zealand, southern South America
2006 March 29	4 min 7 sec	central Africa, Turkey, Russia
2008 August 1	2 min 27 sec	northern Canada, Greenland, Siberia, Mongolia
2009 July 22	6 min 39 sec	eastern Asia, Pacific Ocean
2010 July 11	5 min 20 sec	southern South America

People will sometimes tell you that they once saw a solar eclipse, but cannot remember whether it was partial or total. In that case, it was a partial eclipse. No one who has seen a total solar eclipse has had any doubt, or left the description at a simple, "I saw an eclipse once." During the few minutes preceding totality, as the last sliver of sunlight from the solar disk fights its losing battle with the encroaching moon, the brightness of day disappears with astonishing rapidity. Birds and insects, confused and aroused, change their outpourings of sound. Finally, in just the last few seconds before the total phase of the eclipse, you can look forward to the west and see the moon's shadow rushing at you. As it covers your location, the normal sun disappears completely, revealing what is always there but never otherwise seen, the sun's pearl-white corona, a ring of light around the sun produced by gas heated to a million degrees within the corona. Close to the edge of the sun's disk, orange tongues of hot gas, called solar prominences, thrust themselves toward the corona. The corona bathes the ground with an unearthly light, sometimes including mysterious bands of shadow that race over the land.

Whatever you do, should you be fortunate to see a total solar eclipse, do not spend this time solely in photographing the amazing sight, still less in noting its effect on the local inhabitants, who may, in accordance with tradition, engage in a variety of gestures to make the darkness come to an end. Instead, drink as deeply as you can of the event, urging time to stop, though it will not. No total solar eclipse lasts more than eight minutes twenty seconds, and most bring totality for only two or three minutes; the difference

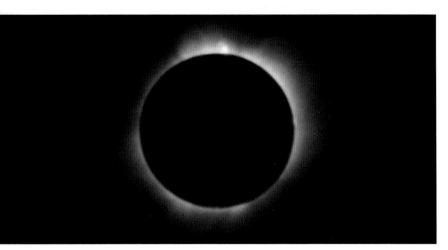

A photograph of a total solar eclipse taken with a telephoto lens reveals orange "prominences" of hot gas protruding above the sun's surface.

arises primarily from changes in the distance from the Earth to the moon, which can vary by plus or minus 5 percent.

MEDITATION

As humanity explored the worlds that orbit the sun, first with telescopes and then with space probes, the moon's special position has grown evermore evident. Except for Pluto, no other planet has a moon nearly so large as ours, in proportion to the planet's own size. Jupiter, Saturn, and Neptune have larger satellites than we do, but these giant planets are so much larger than the Earth that they dwarf all their moons. Pluto, basically a dirty, giant ball of ice and frozen carbon dioxide, does have a comparatively large moon, but because Pluto itself is smaller than our own moon, a second dirty snowball commands little respect.

Thus, among the sun's nine planets, Earth stands out on the basis of having a satellite one-quarter of its own size, when no other (save Pluto) has one even one-tenth as large as itself. Of the sun's inner planets, Mercury and Venus have no moons, while Mars has two, but so small that they cast no significant shadow on their planet. We could easily survive without a large satellite, lacking only some height in the tides (and the biological loss that would entail), an item of poetic inspiration, a source of nighttime illumination, and an obvious though maddening way to subdivide the year. Anything else? Some speculation exists that without a large moon, the tilt of the Earth's axis would undergo large fluctuations, so that the seasonal variations would sometimes be much less than they are now, and at other times much more pronounced. This may or may not be true, and in any case one may speculate that since the Earth's equatorial regions are relatively unaffected by the seasons, life on Earth would always have been able to develop and to evolve over at least part of our planet's surface.

One more favor bestowed by the moon reminds us of our cosmic luck: the eclipses of the sun. If the moon were much closer than it is now, it would cover the sun too fully, plunging the Earth into total darkness below its shadow by covering up not only the sun's disk but also its amazing milk-white corona. On the other hand, if the moon's average distance from Earth were even 4 percent greater than it is now, total solar eclipses could never occur.

The previous two sentences describe the past and future moon. Although the formation of the moon remains in large part mysterious, astronomers now believe that a giant impact with Earth, at the time when our planet was completing its formation, blasted debris into space that orbited the Earth and agglomerated to form our moon. This took place at a distance well under half the moon's present distance from Earth. Since the time of its formation, 4.6 billion years ago, the moon has been slowly but steadily receding from Earth, a process that will continue for billions of years into the future.

What makes the moon recede from Earth? The answer lies in the tides that move water across the sea bottoms. The moon's tide-raising effect on Earth has an effect on the moon itself, changing its angular momentum in orbit with the result that every year sees the moon move a few inches farther from Earth. A quick calculation then shows that only a few hundred million years separate our era from the time when the moon will be too far away to produce a total eclipse of the sun.

The moral seems clear: our successors will envy us for the cosmic spectacles that they can no longer see. Nature has fitted the Earth with a fine coincidence in the sizes and distances of the sun and moon, which turns out to involve a third coincidence, the one in time that gives special effect to the first two. Two or three billion years from now, when strange creatures have taken our places as the dominant species on Earth, they may refer to this epoch not as the time when intelligence developed rapidly, or when humans first left this planet, but rather as the era of solar eclipses. Or could it be that they will have forgotten us entirely? In any case, we can revel in total eclipses of the sun, but they will have no such luck.

Chapter *Three*

Morning Star, Evening Star

This photograph, taken at the Mauna Kea Observatory in Hawaii, captures Venus above the crescent moon as they come close to setting in the west.

"Star light, star bright; first star I see tonight."

What is the first star you see as sundown turns into dusk, and the lights of heaven become visible? If you are looking toward the western horizon, the most likely candidate for the first star in the gloaming, the brightest of all the "stars" in the sky, is not a star at all but the planet Venus.

For more than four and a half billion years, ever since the sun formed along with its planets, Venus has shone its pale yellow light on Earth. Countless generations of humans have marveled at this planet, often assigning it a role in bringing beauty and order to the heavens, just as the reddish color of Mars has suggested blood, disorder, and war. From ancient Mesopotamia, where Venus was known first as Inanna and then as Ishtar, to the Mayans of the Yucatan peninsula three millennia later, many a society has ranked Venus at the top of the list of the celestial objects that rule the Earth below. The Aztecs in Mexico identified Venus with the feathered serpent god Quetzalcoatl, and suffered from an unhappy misidentification of Hernán Cortes with this deity in 1519, when the Spanish conquistadors arrived from the east, the same direction where Venus rose above the waters before dawn. When you see Venus, you bind yourself to a long and glorious mythology.

Venus alternates evenly between her appearances as a "morning star," rising before the sun in the predawn hours, and as an "evening star," setting after the sun does in the dusk. Whether a morning star or an evening star, Venus always appears relatively close to the sun on the sky, a restriction that occurs because Venus orbits the sun *inside* the Earth's orbit, at only 72 percent of the Earth-sun distance. This limits Venus's position on the sky to locations no more than 48 degrees from the sun. As we saw in Chapter 1, a handy guide to measuring angles on the sky resides in your hand and arm: if you stretch out your hand at arm's length, the angle between the tips of your thumb and forefinger, as you see them, equals about 15 degrees. In addition, the angle between the tips of your outstretched thumb and little finger comes close to 20 degrees. Since your fist held at arm's length spans 10 degrees, you hold in your hand an easy way to measure 10, 15, or 20 degrees on the sky.

As Venus orbits the sun, we see it first on one side of the sun and then on the other, either as a "morning star" that rises before the sun does, or as an "evening star" that sets after the sun. The ancient Greeks called Venus "Hesperus" when the planet appeared as the evening star and "Phosphorus" when it was the morning star. The great sage Pythagoras is credited with the realization that Hesperus and Phosphorus must be the same object, which the Greeks later named Aphrodite, whose Roman equivalent was Venus, the goddess of love. In alternating between morning and evening star, and in never moving far from the sun, Venus's motions in the sky differ notably from those of the planets more distant from the sun than Earth, such as Mars and Jupiter. The planets that orbit outside the Earth's orbit can reach positions on the sky as far as 180 degrees from the sun. At these times, called "opposition," the planet lies in the direction opposite to the sun, and therefore, like the full moon, rises at sunset, stays up all night, and sets at sunrise. Venus and Mercury, the planets closer to the sun than Earth, never reach anything close to opposition; instead, they can only oscillate back and forth with respect to the sun, never straying far from the ruler of our heavens.

To achieve its most excellent brightness, Venus intercepts about two parts in a billion of the sun's light. The planet's bright atmosphere reflects about 60 percent of this incoming sunlight, amounting to just over one part in a billion, back into space in different directions. Of this minuscule fraction of the sun's total radiance, about one part in a billion, on the average, reaches the Earth. Yet the fact that we receive barely more than the billionth part of a billionth of the sun's total output suffices to make Venus the third-brightest object in the sky, ranking only behind the sun and moon, when the planet achieves its maximum brilliance. At those times, Venus can cast a shadow, and draws sufficient attention among those who rarely observe the heavens to rank a runaway first among the celestial objects most often reported as UFOs.

Activity One:
Finding Venus

How do you find Venus in the sky? Because the sun's planets continuously move in their orbits around the sun, this question has no answer so simple as the explanations of how to find the Big Dipper or any

other group of stars. Instead, locating Venus assumes the aspect of finding a ballroom dancer on a crowded floor when you are also one of the dancers. With both the Earth and Venus in orbital motion around the sun, Venus wanders in a complex way against the background of stars, so that we cannot say, as we can for the stars, "On this particular day of the year, look for Venus in a particular direction." If you want to obsess on the difficulty of figuring out how to find Venus, imagine yourself on a visit to a beautiful city park, where an antique merry-go-round occupies the center of a large clearing amidst the trees. Seat yourself on one of the horses that line the merry-go-round's outer edge, and let it whirl you in a circular motion around a stationary center, which we may call the sun. Then you mimic the Earth's yearly orbit, and, as you look toward the center of the merry-go-round, you will note that the sun appears against a changing background of faraway trees, which represent the starry heavens. But unlike a garden-variety merry-go-round, this solar-system model does not possess a solid, rotating floor. Instead, the animals mounted closer to the sun take less time to circle the center than you do. Every time that you make one trip around the sun, the interior line of animals makes more than a trip and a half. Together, these interior animals trace out the orbit of Venus, and one of them marks the planet itself. You can then easily conclude that the task of following the motions of Venus, either against the backdrop of distant stars or with respect to the sun at the center of the merry-go-round, is not the child's play it would be if only the Earth stood still.

In older societies, determining the motions of Venus and the other planets, so that the high priests could know with confidence where to find them at all times, occupied the top position on the list of an astronomer's tasks, along with following the paths of the sun and moon and predicting eclipses of ill omen. Today, we well understand the basic principles behind these determinations, and have created computers that can calculate the planets' positions in the sky to an accuracy finer than anything the best telescope can see. These computers have programs that solve the puzzle of the planetary merry-go-round, and even allow for the fact that the planets' orbits are ellipses, not perfect circles. As a result, each planet moves slightly more rapidly when closer to the sun, slightly more slowly when farther away. For purposes of finding the planets, what counts is that the computer programs, like astronomers of old with pen and ink, can accurately predict where to find each planet at any time in the future.

Because these positions do not recur on a yearly cycle, it would be useless to describe how to find Venus in the fall, the spring, or any other season: one year's accurate description would become the next year's complete catastrophe. Instead, we must take Venus where she is and will be, specifying her position with respect to the sun. The best way to do this is to list the months in each year when Venus will be visible either before sunrise or after sunset, along with the date when Venus appears on the sky farthest from the sun, and therefore either sets at the latest or rises at the earliest possible time. We then create what we might call a Venusian calendar, presented on the next page. This calendar summarizes the changing positions of Venus, and shows that during the months when the planet is neither a morning star nor an evening star, Venus will be passing either almost directly between the Earth and the sun, or almost directly behind the sun. As a result, we cannot see Venus at all at these times without binoculars or even finer optical equipment. Because this calendar provides only one position per month (appropriately enough, this marks Venus's position at the middle of that month), we must use some extrapolation for other dates, noting whether Venus is moving farther from the sun or closer toward the sun.

If you find yourself in one of the good periods for observing Venus, take yourself to a place with a good western view about an hour after sunset (when Venus is an evening star) or find a good eastern view about an hour before sunrise (when Venus is a morning star). For this activity, you won't have to escape the city's lights, or wait for a time when the moon is down; all you need is your eyes and a sky free from clouds. You should find Venus with no difficulty at all, and if Venus is an evening star, you can verify that you have done so by waiting for complete darkness and making sure that Venus shines more brightly than any star. The only real danger of confusion arises from aircraft, which can be easily distinguished from planets by waiting half a minute to see whether the bright object moves in the sky.

With a mere glance at the sky, together with a look at the Venusian calendar, you can thus easily find Venus, shining brightly with light reflected by its atmosphere, which consists (we now know) mainly of carbon dioxide, so thick that the heat trapped by Venus's atmosphere almost melts the rocks on its surface. By finding Venus, you have joined the elite group of those who know a planet when they see one.

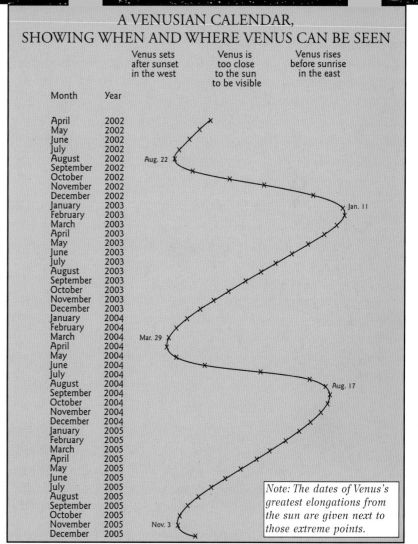

A VENUSIAN CALENDAR, SHOWING WHEN AND WHERE VENUS CAN BE SEEN

Note: The dates of Venus's greatest elongations from the sun are given next to those extreme points.

The "Venusian Calendar" also demonstrates, in a rough-and-ready manner, the different speeds at which Venus changes its position with respect to the sun. You can see, for example, that only four months and twenty days (twice seventy-one days) pass between Venus's greatest western elongation on August 22, 2002, when the planet sets nearly three hours after the sun does, and its greatest eastern elongation on January 11, 2003, when Venus rises almost three hours before the sun. During that time, Venus speeds ahead of the Earth in its orbit, passing almost directly between the Earth and the sun at the halfway point of those 142 days. Venus then takes more than three times as long, or 442 days, to perform the other half of its swing, around the far side of the sun, moving from its greatest eastern elongation on January 11, 2003 to its greatest western elongation on March 29, 2004. In analyzing the speeds with which Venus seems to approach or recede from the sun on the sky, we can see that the reversals of direction of Venus's motion that occur at the planet's two points of greatest elongation from the sun on the sky separate the periods of Venus's most rapid motion with respect to the sun from those of its slowest movement.

TWINKLE, TWINKLE

When you observe Venus, note that the planet shines with a steadier light than the stars do, barely twinkling while the stars wink and sparkle in the skies. Why so? Because Venus, even though far smaller than any star, lies so much closer to us than the stars do that we can see the planet as more than a point of light. The twinkling of the stars arises whenever a beam of starlight passes through Earth's atmosphere and inevitably receives multiple small refractions by different pockets of air, each of which deviates the beam by a tiny amount. Since air currents prevent the atmosphere from ever remaining totally still, the changing refractions continuously make the star's position in the sky seem to dance. In contrast, Venus exhibits almost none of this, because our eyes receive light rays reflected from different parts of the planet's disk simultaneously. As each of these light rays undergoes multiple refractions, their effects, which occur more or less at random, tend to cancel one another. This keeps Venus glowing much more steadily than the pointlike stars—another good way to make sure that you have found Venus and not a bright star.

If you have an excellent pair of binoculars, you can actually see the disk of Venus, which exhibits phases similar to the moon's as it moves around its orbit. Venus has a diameter almost as large as Earth's, and nearly four times the moon's, but because Venus—even at its closest to Earth—has a distance more than a hundred times the distance to the moon, Venus can never appear even $\frac{1}{25}$ as large as the moon, and our unaided eyes see Venus only as a single bright spot of light. As Venus changes its position with respect to ourselves and the sun, we see the progression of its phases by observing changing fractions of its sunlit and dark hemispheres. At its greatest distance from the sun on the sky, Venus shows us about half of each hemisphere; when it is much closer to the sun, on the parts of its orbit that bring it nearly between the sun and Earth, binoculars will show Venus as only a thin crescent. But this crescent is much larger than the half-Venus we see at Venus's greatest elongation from the sun, because Venus is much closer to us. When Galileo first used a telescope to observe Venus, he discovered these changing phases of our sister planet, which he announced to the world in a cryptic anagram, the decipherment of which said (in Latin), "the mother of loves imitates the changes of the moon."

Too Hot!

In terms of the planets' evolution and fitness for life, Earth plays the central role in a scenario that might be called "Goldilocks and the Three Planets." So far as life goes, Venus is far too hot, Mars is a bit too cold, and Earth is just right.

Venus's high temperature arises in part because it orbits closer to the sun, at just 72 percent of the Earth's distance. But Venus's pale yellow glow hides another fact that makes the planet far hotter than we might expect: a thick, stifling blanket of carbon-dioxide gas, almost a hundred times thicker than Earth's atmosphere. Because carbon-dioxide molecules block infrared radiation with great efficiency, these molecules trap the heat that a planet receives from the sun. This solar heating arrives in the form of visible light that warms the planet's surface, which glows with infrared radiation. When this radiation attempts to escape, it finds itself blocked by the carbon dioxide in an atmosphere so dense that the pressure on Venus's surface equals the crushing pressure that a deep-sea diver would feel half a mile below the ocean surface. Earth's atmosphere, made mostly of nitrogen and oxygen, also contains some carbon-dioxide and water-vapor molecules, which likewise trap heat radiated by the surface; this keeps our planet 10 to 20 degrees warmer than it would be in the absence of an atmosphere. On Venus, however, the trapping of heat by carbon dioxide—ten thousand times more carbon dioxide than we find in the Earth's atmosphere!—raises the temperature not by tens of degrees but by the best part of a thousand degrees, so that Venus's entire surface, dayside, nightside, and twilight, roasts at 900 degrees Fahrenheit!

In short, carbon dioxide has made Venus a close approximation to a vision of hell. Like a demon, the planet's lovely appearance from afar hides what we would consider infernal conditions on the surface. We would do well to remember the lesson of Venus as we perform the experiment of seeing what will happen as the result of increasing the carbon-dioxide content of our own atmosphere.

Activity Two:
Following Venus on Its Path around the Sun

Once you have located Venus in the skies on a particular day, either shortly before dawn or soon after sunrise, you will have no difficulty in finding Venus on the days immediately afterward. If you let time slip, however, you may be surprised by the speed with which Venus can change its position with respect to the sun and the stars. Of all the planets, only quicksilver Mercury, much dimmer than Venus and much more difficult to find because it always lies so close to the sun on the sky, moves more rapidly than Venus does. As you observe Venus during the course of a few weeks, you will acquire a good feeling of how the planet is moving; if you extend your observations over a few months, you can connect with ancient astronomers, who recorded the motions of the brightest planet and sought to understand them, often by imposing a mental framework that failed to fit the basic facts about the solar system.

In changing its distance from the sun on the sky, Venus exhibits two sorts of motions: fairly rapid and extremely rapid. The distinction arises from the fact that Venus's distance from Earth varies enormously as Venus moves in orbit. In terms of the cosmic merry-go-round in which the sun occupies the center, we sometimes see the planet close to us, passing almost directly between ourselves and the sun, and at other times observe Venus moving through the distant parts of its orbit, at distances six times greater than its distance at the time of its closest approach to the Earth, which astronomers call "inferior conjunction."

Venus takes only 7.25 months to circle the sun. During this time, however, the Earth moves more than halfway around its own orbit, so Venus must spend considerably longer, and in fact must orbit the sun more than two and a half times, before regaining its original position with respect to the sun and Earth. Since Venus moves more rapidly in its orbit than Earth does, and since it has a lesser distance to cover in each orbit, it can indeed catch up with and overtake the Earth, but only after a relatively long contest. After each inferior conjunction of Venus, for example, the next one occurs not 7.25 months afterward but for a full year longer that that: a total of 584 days, equal to 1 year, 7 months, and 9 days, must elapse before Venus once again makes its closest approach to Earth.

At and near the times of its inferior conjunction, Venus becomes invisible, since its dark side then faces the Earth, and Venus rises and sets along with the sun, close to it on the sky and therefore lost in the sun's glare. A week or ten days after its inferior conjunction, Venus makes its first appearance as the morning star, close to the sun and visible only shortly before dawn.

During the next eight or nine weeks, you can see Venus move progressively farther from the sun on the sky, so that it rises each morning earlier than the sun does. Venus is now moving at its most rapid pace with respect to the sun, because the planet is coursing through the parts of its orbit closest to Earth: its steady speed in orbit gives Venus a comparatively quick gait on the sky, just as a deer flushed from the woods at close range moves far more rapidly across our field of view than one seen several hundred yards away.

Moving, then, with all deliberate speed against the backdrop of stars, Venus not only rises progressively sooner than the sun, but also grows steadily brighter, because it exposes more and more of its sunlit hemisphere to our view. Each successive day will show you a new position and a different brightness for Venus. Only seventy-one days elapse from the time of Venus's inferior conjunction to the morning when Venus reaches its greatest elongation, its largest distance from the sun on the sky, close to 48 degrees. On this day, Venus rises almost three hours earlier than the sun. By the time of its greatest elongation, Venus has already passed its moment of maximum brightness, which occurs a few weeks earlier and gives Venus twenty times the brightness of any star. But at its greatest elongation, Venus rises at its earliest and glows with a majestic brightness, because its greater distance from the sun on the sky makes it even more prominent in the predawn skies. The days near its greatest elongation offer the finest and easiest opportunities to observe our planetary neighbor, for Venus then shines nearly as brightly as it can and rises as long before sunrise as is possible.

After its day of greatest elongation as a "morning star," Venus starts to reduce its distance from the sun on the sky. However, since the planet is now moving through parts of its orbit that lie at progressively greater distances from the Earth, we see Venus slow its motion on the sky with respect to the sun. Venus also grows dimmer, because even though we see a greater fraction of its sunlit half, the planet's increasing distance from Earth results in a lesser brightness for our sister planet. Fully four months will pass, with Venus dimmer and closer to the sun every day before dawn, until our sister planet passes almost directly behind the sun, in what astronomers denote as its superior conjunction. During the last weeks of

these four months, Venus again becomes invisible, because it lies in a direction on the sky too close to the sun for us to discern the planet amid the solar blaze.

When Venus reaches its superior conjunction, the farthest point from Earth along its orbit, the planet makes the transition from morning star to evening star. Several weeks more must elapse, however, before you can see Venus again, this time in the glow of dusk, as Venus follows the sun in setting by half an hour or so. The months after superior conjunction play the same scenes for Venus as before, but in reverse order and in the skies after sunset. First Venus makes its appearance in the evening skies, still relatively dim but nevertheless brighter than any star. Then, during the next four months, Venus slowly moves farther from the sun on the sky, growing ever brighter and setting at progressively longer intervals after sunset, until its greatest elongation as an evening star occurs when Venus once again stands fully 47 or 48 degrees away from the sun, and sets some three hours after sunset, unmistakably the brightest starlike object in the heavens. Following its greatest elongation, Venus moves much more rapidly during the next seventy-one days, growing ever closer to the sun in the sky, first passing through its moment of maximum brightness and then quickly losing visibility as it grows both dimmer and closer to the sun as we see it. Finally, Venus will reach inferior conjunction, just 584 days after its previous one. The next seventy-one days will again see Venus moving rapidly away from the sun, making the planet ever more prominent in the skies before dawn.

To most of us, the 584 days that pass during a full cycle of Venus's motion on the sky, from one inferior conjunction to the next, are just another astronomical number to keep track of if we are in the mood. But to ancient astronomers, this number seemed almost mystical, because five full cycles of Venus's motion occur within the span of 2,920 days, which almost equals eight full years (8 x 365.25 = 2,922). In other words, the lengths of the seasons of a year on Earth and of the Venus cycle on the sky stand in a ratio of nearly 5 to 8, as if a cosmic mathematician had been at work, inventing the cyclical motions of the heavens to impress us with the fact that every fifth cycle of Venus's motion begins just about eight years later, at nearly the same season of the year as the first one.

In fact, this near-match between the motions of Venus and the Earth is simply a cosmic coincidence, not quite perfect, since five cycles of Venus's motion leave us two days out of place in the yearly calendar. The cycles of Venus received high honors from the ancient Chaldeans and the Mayans, who knew how to honor the brightest of the planets, even if their reasons would not withstand modern scrutiny. When you follow Venus through the 584-day cycle of its motion with respect to the sun, you link yourself both to our intellectual history and to the solar system, whose motions provide the cosmic clocks that fascinated our ancestors.

Activity Three:
The Transits of Venus

Of all the phenomena associated with observations of Venus, the rarest are its transits across the sun, the days when Venus's inferior conjunction brings the planet precisely between ourselves and the solar disk. If Venus had an enormous size, instead of a diameter just 95 percent as large as the Earth's, these transits would noticeably diminish the amount of sunlight reaching the Earth. Because Venus has a diameter less than 1 percent of the sun's, however, a transit of Venus reduces the amount of sunlight shining on Earth by less than one part in ten thousand, making these events insignificant—except to those who care.

Why doesn't a transit occur every 584 days, at each of Venus's inferior conjunctions? The answer lies in the fact that Venus's orbit around the sun does not lie in precisely the same plane as the Earth's orbit. Instead, the two planes are slightly tilted, by an angle of about 3.5 degrees, so that Venus passes a bit above or below the sun at most inferior conjunctions, rather than directly across it. A similar tilt in the plane of the moon's orbit around the Earth keeps us from the boredom of a total solar eclipse at every new moon; instead, solar eclipses occur somewhere on Earth only once or twice each year.

For Venus, only about one inferior conjunction in every fifty produces a transit. Transits of Venus come in pairs, spaced eight years apart. The most recent transits of Venus (on December 9, 1874 and December 6, 1882) no longer exist in personal memories; the next two, on June 8, 2004 and June 6, 2012, offer a twice-in-a-lifetime chance to see an exceedingly rare astronomical event. Note that the eight-year interval between transits corresponds to the five cycles of Venus's motion with respect to the sun, which we described above.

Once upon a time, the transits of Venus played an important role in measuring the solar system. Astronomers at two or more widely separated locations on Earth who precisely measured and timed the moments when the transit began and ended could use trigonometry to work out the distance to the sun. To achieve this result required expeditions to far-off corners of the globe, which involved some astronomers in Herculean efforts that ring through the ages, at least among their astronomical descendants. Every young astronomer for generations has heard the story of the French astronomer Guillaume-Joseph-Hyacinthe-Jean-Baptiste Le Gentil de la Galaisière, usually known simply as Le Gentil, which astronomical elders recount to show what astronomy was like in the old days. Le Gentil was sent to observe the transit of Venus of June 1761 from Pondicherry, the French enclave in India. He left France in March 1760, but what with the difficulty of ocean voyages and the need to avoid British warships (for a worldwide conflict was then raging between France and England, the war that bears the American name, oddly, of the "French and Indian

War") was still at sea fifteen months later; his fine view of the transit was therefore useless to science, for a boat rolls far too much to permit highly accurate observations.

After due consideration, Le Gentil decided that rather than rush home, he would prepare for the transit of June 1769, already less than eight years in the future. And so he did, exploring as far as Madagascar and the Philippines, learning a good deal about Africa and Asia, and vacillating between Manila and Pondicherry as the best site from which to observe the coming transit. Pondicherry won the contest, so Le Gentil returned to India, where (peace having broken out) he received assistance from the British as well as the French in preparing for his observations. Unfortunately, the day of the transit in 1769 proved to be cloudy in Pondicherry (though brilliantly clear in Manila), so the two transits yielded Le Gentil no scientific results at all. Somewhat discouraged, he set out for home, almost succumbing to dysentery and shipwreck during an eighteen-month voyage that included a four-month stay on a nearly deserted islet. Returning to France after almost a dozen years away, Le Gentil discovered that he had long been presumed dead, his seat in the Académie Royale

des Sciences had been assigned to another, and his heirs were quarreling over his estate—a situation that gave Le Gentil, still in his mid-thirties, plenty to do in order to resume a normal life, which, we may happily report, he promptly did. Fortunately for science, other world travelers, including Charles Mason and Jeremiah Dixon (of Mason-Dixon fame) at the Cape of Good Hope in Africa, had successfully made accurate observations of the transit of 1769. These results yielded the most accurate determination of the sun's distance for more than a century.

Le Gentil's travels and the history of the transits of 1761 and 1769 share a key fact with the coming transits of 2004 and 2012, one that affects your ability to see them in the most practical way: like the two transits of Venus in the eighteenth century, the two of the early twenty-first century will be visible only from the Old World, not the New. If you want to enjoy one of these two events, you must go to Europe, Africa, or Asia, because only the last few minutes of the transit of 2004, which will last for more than five hours, will be visible from the easternmost United States, and none of the transit of 2012. You must also arrange for optical equipment that will project the sun's disk through a telescope onto a flat plane of white cardboard or metal, for it is too dangerous to rely on a sun filter inside the telescope for direct viewing. Be sure, if you do go, to pick a place that offers good weather prospects so you can avoid the fate of Le Gentil, who, after all his efforts, failed in his mission because of a cloud cover. Of course, you will travel much more easily than he did, and perhaps the adventure of such a trip will be a reward in itself.

MEDITATION

Now that you have learned how to find Venus in the sky, and have come to appreciate the rhythms by which Venus exchanges its roles as morning star and evening star, you are poised to take the crucial step that separates feeling from understanding. Like generations of sky watchers before you, consider the deep and puzzling question, Why does Venus appear as it does in our skies?

For millennia, this question received an answer that made good sense to everyone who pondered it. Venus constantly changes its position in the sky because it is moving—a conclusion that turns out to be absolutely true, an example of successful deduction. But *how* does Venus move? This part of the issue received an answer that became ever more subtle, but had at its root a simple assumption: Venus moves on an orbit around the *Earth*. All of our observation testifies that the sun, moon, stars, and planets move through our skies; the more you observe these objects, the more evident it becomes that they move while we stand below them, on solid, unmoving earth. To reach conclusions about the cosmos on the basis of this experience makes perfectly good sense. Throughout recorded history, all astronomical hypotheses about the motions of Venus have begun with the notion that Venus continuously moves around the Earth.

What form does this motion take? To ancient Greek astronomers, the answer had to lie in a single type of curve, the perfect circle. This conclusion stood not on experience of the natural world, but rather on a longing for perfection, which nature simply ought to express. No form seemed as perfect as a circle, whose every point has the same distance from its center. If this is so, and if nature radiates perfection, then the motions of objects in the cosmos should be circular. This belief occupies the starting point of astronomical hypotheses about the motions of Venus, and of all the other planets as well.

But the Greeks also knew how to observe nature. Like those who lived elsewhere, they studied the heavens and recorded the changing positions of Venus. They soon saw, as you will too, that grave problems arise in explaining what we see, if we assume that Venus moves in a circle around Earth. In that case, Venus must always have the same distance from Earth. Why, then, does Venus change its brightness? Today we might attempt to answer this question by asserting that Venus draws its brightness from sunlight, and that the distance from the sun to Venus could change as each of these objects moved around the Earth. To ancient astronomers, however, the issue of Venus's brightness did not draw much attention, perhaps for the excellent reason that no good theory existed of how an object's brightness changed as its distance from the source of illumination. Ancient astronomers concentrated far more on the fundamental issue of Venus's changing positions in the sky. Here, too, an enormous problem arises if we assume that Venus moves around the Earth at a constant speed. In that case, we should likewise see Venus changing its position at a constant speed. This simply does not occur: we have seen that Venus sometimes moves relatively slowly, maintaining nearly the same position for weeks on end, and at other times seems to dart across the sky in a gait that sharply contrasts with its slow-footed waltz. Furthermore, we have seen that the periods of relatively fast and slow motion alternate, one supplanting the other in a cyclical manner. How can we explain this?

The ancient Greeks might have concluded that Venus moves on its circular orbit with a speed that varies at different points along this orbit. However, this conclusion had absolutely no appeal to them, because it violated the same notion of perfection that the circle expressed. A perfect object would not only move in a circle but would also do so at a constant speed; deviations from a constant velocity could no more be accepted than deviations from motion in circles. What, then, could be done to reconcile the notion of circular perfection with the observed motion of the planet Venus?

Lesser minds might well have concluded that there was no answer. Given the experience recorded in the observations of Venus, the hypothesis of circular motion at a constant velocity could not be maintained. But the supple minds of ancient Greek astronomers conceived a way out. Instead of a single circle, they conceived of several circles. To the original circular orbit of Venus, they added a smaller circle, called an *epicycle*. They imagined that what was moving in a great circle around Earth at a constant speed was not Venus itself, but rather a point in space, the center of Venus's epicycle. Venus itself moved in a circle around this point at a constant speed, maintaining a distance from the epicycle's center considerably smaller than the size of the epicycle's circular orbit.

Close your eyes and imagine what the astronomers had invented: a wheel within a wheel, the small wheel turning twice as fast as the large one, so that as the center of the small wheel circled the Earth, the planet Venus, moving around this wheel, changed both its distance from Earth and the speed at which it moved through the sky. At some times, the motion of Venus on its epicycle had the same direction as the motion of the epicycle's center around the Earth. At other times, however, Venus moved on its epicycle in the direction opposite to the epicycle's large motion around us. Thus, Venus's epicyclic speed sometimes added to, and sometimes subtracted from, the speed of the epicycle's center.

Impressively, with this model of the cosmos, the astronomers succeeded in calculating Venus's changing speeds and positions. They found that the model provided fairly good agreement with the positions and motions of Venus that they observed—good, but not exact. To astronomers hooked on allowing only circular motion at a constant speed, only one way out of this difficulty beckoned: more circles. When the epicyclic theory of Venus's motion reached its apex, half a dozen additional epicycles had been added, each of them a smaller circle that took the planet on an excursion from a larger one. That is, not only did the astronomers conceive of an epicycle whose center moved in a circular orbit around the Earth; they also imagined smaller epicycles, whose centers performed circular orbits around a point on the large orbit!

There is an important lesson here. Scientific understanding of the cosmos proceeds through a combination of observational experience and the ability to form models, mental projections that embody certain notions of how things ought to behave. Through the interplay of observation with these models—theories of the cosmos, if we choose that term—we can learn whether the models make sense. We learn more than that, however. The models teach us to ask, What is really happening in the cosmos? How does it all fit together? And to inquire, just as our forebears did, where do we fit in?

Chapter *Four*

Follow the Drinking Gourd

As the Earth rotates, every star that lies north of the celestial equator on the sky appears to move in a circular path around the north celestial pole.

For many millennia, humans have navigated by the stars, using their motions to find the north point on the horizon, and with it, the other cardinal points of the compass. Today, few of us know this technique, and someone who uses the expression "True North" is probably referring to a spiritual or emotional path. If you seek to reconnect with our astronomical roots, there is no finer way to begin than with a look to the north. For centuries, seafarers have used the North Star to guide them across the seas. Tonight, you can locate the North Star by using the Big Dipper, and use it to navigate through your neighborhood. You may be surprised at how easy this can be, as well as at how thoroughly our technological prowess has robbed us of skills as simple as determining the basic directions that describe how we can travel.

Once you have learned to find the Big Dipper easily, you can use it to locate other constellations, and even to tell time by the stars. Thus of all the stars that shine in the skies of night, the seven that form the Big Dipper have proven the most useful, not only in past eras but on every clear evening when you might want to find the way north.

Activity One:
To Know the Big Dipper

Every night, as the Earth rotates silently beneath us, the Big Dipper's seven stars appear to wheel around the point on the sky that astronomers call the north celestial pole. This celestial pole marks the location on the sky that happens to lie directly above the Earth's North Pole, so that as the Earth turns, this point remains motionless while the rest of the sky rotates around it. Polaris, the North Star, lies almost at the north celestial pole, and the Big Dipper will help you find it. Your first task therefore consists of locating the Dipper itself.

Because the Big Dipper's stars all lie relatively close to the north celestial pole, their slow wheel never carries any of them below the horizon for most northern-hemisphere viewers. In the southernmost United States, part of the Big Dipper does set briefly below the northern horizon, but only for an hour or two. We can therefore say fairly that on almost any clear night, you can see the Big Dipper from anywhere in the United States, and this is absolutely true for anyone living as far north as San Francisco or Philadelphia. Look for seven stars of nearly equal brightness, three in the Dipper's handle and four that form its bowl. To be sure that you have the right seven stars, stretch your hand out at arm's length in front of the Dipper's handle. The distance on the sky from the star at the far tip of the handle to the star in the bowl of the Dipper farthest from the handle should equal 20 degrees, the span of your outstretched hand between the tip of your thumb and the tip of your little finger, making the Big Dipper a large constellation, though not the largest in the sky.

When using the Big Dipper to find north, you follow an ancient procedure, drawing on sky lore, known to humans for thousands of years. In Homer's *Odyssey*, the siren Calypso tells Odysseus always to keep the Big Dipper (that is, the direction northward) on his left as he sails the Mediterranean Sea, so that his course will continue to carry him eastward. Today, with city lights dimming our views of the night sky, and with the heavens above no longer such a seemingly dominant player in the game of life, we take the stars for granted. Yet the Big Dipper continues to lie above us, wheeling each night around the pole of the sky, available to show us the way to the north. The fact that we now understand the composition, the distances, and the motions of the Dipper's stars simply enhances rather than diminishes their luster. If you want to know the stars of night, the starting point remains as it was three millennia ago: find the Big Dipper.

NAMES OF STARS IN THE BIG DIPPER

Dubhe and Merak, the two stars farthest from the Big Dipper's handle, are the "Pointers" that show the way to Polaris, the North Star.

THE OTHER NAMES OF URSA MAJOR

To various cultures, the Big Dipper's seven stars have suggested more than a drinking gourd or a dipper made for the same purpose. Of all the constellations, the Big Dipper carries the most variegated set of names in the history of English-speaking peoples. In Britain and Ireland, you will hear the Dipper called the Plough, since its shape resembles what we in America call a plow; in addition, you can sometimes hear the old name of Charles's Wain (Charles's Wagon), which apparently arose from a legendary association of King Arthur with Charlemagne. Certainly the Plough looks like a wagon with a long tongue, and was called the wagon throughout much of Europe in bygone eras.

Most intriguing of all the names for the Big Dipper is the Great Bear, which in Latin, as Ursa Major, gives the constellation its official name. Imagining these stars to form a giant bear in the sky occurred not only in Europe (the Greeks in Homer's time called the constellation Arktos, meaning the Bear) but also among many of the native American tribes. George Bancroft, the famous nineteenth-century American historian, wrote that "It is a curious coincidence, that among the Algonquians of the Atlantic and the Mississippi, alike among the Narragansett and the Illinois, the North Star was called the Bear." (Bancroft must have confused the Big Dipper, which points to the North Star, with the star itself.)

Activity Two:
Navigate by the Big Dipper

Now that you have located the Big Dipper, take a walk in your neighborhood under the clear night skies. Plan on walking for about an hour, but adapt your expedition to your own convenience. First walk north for fifteen minutes, following the Big Dipper. Depending on your immediate neighborhood, you may find yourself having to turn corners and to zigzag your way toward the north, or you may find a clear, open road that bends toward the Big Dipper. In either case, try to imagine yourself on a journey, traveling to parts unknown, reachable only by staying on your course. When you have gone as far north as you can in your allotted time, turn and walk to the east for fifteen minutes, using the Dipper again as your compass by keeping it on your left hand. Then turn south for fifteen minutes, walking directly away from the Dipper, and finally turn to the west, keeping the Dipper on your right hand, and walk for a final quarter hour. With any luck, you should find yourself back at your own front door. Sit outside for a moment, imagining what it might have been like to travel under the Big Dipper for days or weeks, traveling north to freedom.

FOLLOW THE DRINKING GOURD

A century and a half ago, the scourge of slavery lay heavily on the United States, an evil that corrupted society and our political system. A minuscule number of slaves succeeded in making an incredibly difficult escape to freedom. The perils of such a flight arose not only from the heavy hand of the slave system in the southern states but also from the fact that a federal law required that any fugitive slaves identified in the northern states must be sent back to slave masters in the south. Only by passing all the way through the United States into Canada could a slave become completely free, liberated not only from the condition of slavery but also from the possibility of being handed over to the courts for return southward into bondage.

For the entire slave population, the obstacles to escape included the lack of any possibility of written communication. In many states, a slave risked death for attempting to learn to read, and any messages promoting escape would have led to immediate execution. Forced to rely exclusively on oral interchanges, slaves learned to pass information with seemingly innocuous messages, not least with the songs that their masters loved to hear them sing, often citing them as proof of general content-ment among the slave population. We can imagine a slave owner listening in the evening to one of the finest of these songs, which begins with the lines:

When the sun comes back and the first quail calls,
Follow the drinking gourd!

and includes specific topographical information in its verses, each of which ends with:

Follow the drinking gourd! Follow the drinking gourd!
For the old man is a-waitin' for to carry you to freedom,
If you follow the drinking gourd!

Within this song, with what must have seemed a reference to the heavenly kingdom awaiting the steadfast believer, lies crucial astronomical information: the Drinking Gourd, which we now call the Big Dipper, points the way northward.

Activity Three:
Use the Big Dipper to Find the North Star

To achieve greater precision in locating the north point on your horizon, you must use the Big Dipper to find Polaris, the North Star. To do so, find the two stars in the Dipper's bowl that are farthest from the handle, and draw an imaginary line from the lower through the upper one. (Here "lower" and "upper" refer to the concept that the Big Dipper can be used to lift and to pour liquid, so that the "lower" star lies at the bottom of the four-star bowl and the "upper" star at the top.) For obvious reasons, these two stars are called the "Pointers." If you extend the imaginary line through the two Pointers, moving away from the upper star and continuing for about five times the distance between the Pointers, you will encounter Polaris, a star almost as bright as those in the Dipper.

Because this star happens to lie in the direction almost exactly above the Earth's North Pole, its position in the sky nearly coincides with the north celestial pole, so the star well deserves its Latin name, Polaris, which refers to the North Pole. In English, we often refer to Polaris as the North Star. Since the star lies close to the north celestial pole, the north point on the horizon always lies almost directly downward from Polaris. Even a long-range aircraft cannot go far wrong in using Polaris to determine true north, and for all ordinary purposes, we may regard the agreement in position between Polaris and the north celestial pole as exact.

A WOBBLING PLANET

Because the Earth's axis of rotation slowly wobbles in space, pointing in different directions around the circle of the sky, the location of the north celestial pole wanders in a slow circle among the constellations. For the ancient Egyptians, Polaris could not serve as the "North Star"; instead, Thuban, the brightest star in Draco the Dragon (nowhere nearly as bright as Polaris) filled that role. The wandering of the north celestial pole brings it back to its initial point after a 26,000-year "cycle of precession" has passed. Fourteen thousand years from now, the bright star Vega will serve as humanity's North Star; twelve thousand years after that, Polaris will once again perform this service. For the time being, we can take comfort in the fact that the slow wobble of the Earth's rotation axis will actual move the north celestial pole a bit closer to Polaris during the next few centuries, making Polaris an even finer North Star than it is now, just over 1 degree (twice the moon's apparent diameter) from the north celestial pole. Only after the middle of the new millennium will Polaris begin to lose its pride of place, though it will take several thousand years after that before we must take precautions against identifying Polaris's position on the sky with that of the north celestial pole. We may note with hemispheric chauvinism that no bright star lies near the south celestial pole, the point directly above the Earth's South Pole (see page 175). Observers in the southern hemisphere must therefore make do with other ways to find the south celestial pole—a point that never rises above the horizon for any observer north of the Earth's equator.

The North Star lies at the tip of the handle of the Little Dipper, which also contains seven stars. In comparison with the Big Dipper, however, these stars shine quite modestly, so that only the keen-eyed on a clear night can see them all. (Far from city lights, the task becomes much easier, and all seven stars in the Little Dipper will seem to jump out of the sky in comparison with the city-shrouded view.) On most city nights, only two stars in the Little Dipper can be easily seen: Polaris and the star at the far end of the bowl, called by its Arabic name Kochab. If you have dark skies and the chance to see the rest of the Little Dipper, you will note that its orientation on the sky mirrors that of the Big Dipper; one of the two dippers is always pouring into the other, depending on which one lies above the other in the sky as the Earth turns.

This photograph of the Big Dipper (on the right) and the Little Dipper (above and to the right of the top of the moonlit butte) shows the greater brightness of the Big Dipper's stars, as well as the greater size of the Big Dipper itself. The top two stars in the Big Dipper, called the "Pointers," mark a line toward Polaris, the North Star, at the tip of the handle of the Little Dipper.

OLD LIGHT

Like everything else in the cosmos, the seven stars of the Big Dipper shine with old news. All of astronomy is history: light takes a finite time to travel through space. Even a year of time allows light to travel "only" about six trillion miles—approximately 65,000 times the distance from the Earth to the sun. Astronomers long ago created a unit of distance called the light year, equal to the six trillion miles that light travels in a year, an excellent yardstick except for its name, which often leads to confusion over whether light years measure time or distance.

Astronomers believe that the six stars in the Big Dipper with similar distances (all but Alcaid) were born together as part of a loose cluster called an "association," a conclusion supported by the fact that these six stars are all moving through space in nearly the same direction.

For human purposes, the more immediate "usefulness" of these distances lies in connecting us to the scales of time and distance that characterize the cosmos. The sun and its planets occupy a tiny portion of a far corner of a galaxy of stars that we call the Milky Way. Of the 300 billion or so stars in the Milky Way, a few thousand happen to lie sufficiently close to the solar system, and to shine with sufficiently great intrinsic luminosities, that we can see them at night without optical aid. All of these "naked-eye stars" lie so close to us that if we drew a map of the Milky Way on a sheet of paper, a single small dot would cover all of them. This dot represents our starry neighborhood, the million closest cousins of our sun.

Think for a moment about the messages in time carried by the light from the Big Dipper. Except for Alcaid, the travel time for the light to reach us from each of them corresponds to a long human lifetime, and thus to events that occurred long ago, as we count time, without being so long ago that we cannot easily perceive these intervals of time. The light from Dubhe and Phecda, for example, left on its journey while Theodore Roosevelt was President of the United States, whereas the light from Alioth, Mizar, and Merak was produced during the era of Prohibition and Babe Ruth. In contrast, the light from Alcaid, at the end of the Dipper's handle, has been traveling since the epoch when the Declaration of Independence marked the start of the American Revolution. We see these stars, like everything else in the universe, not as they are but as they were when their light began its journey toward us. Because a few centuries amount to only a blink in cosmic time, however, this view effectively reveals the present situation among the stars. Nevertheless, if any of the Big Dipper's stars should be suddenly snuffed out, a lifetime would pass before the news reached the Earth.

Using these convenient units, we can state some basic facts about the Big Dipper's seven stars:

Star Name	Distance in light years	Energy Output (Sun=1)
Alcaid	227	800
Mizar	85	90
Alioth	82	95
Mergez	92	50
Phecda	100	100
Merak	77	60
Dubhe	98	140

USING THE BIG DIPPER TO FIND OTHER CONSTELLATIONS

In addition to pointing the way north, the Big Dipper provides another great usefulness to astronomy, not so practical but entirely worthwhile nonetheless. The Dipper points the way to neighboring constellations, which in turn can be used to find their neighbors.

We have seen that the Dipper's two pointer stars, which form the end of the Dipper's bowl, invariably point toward Polaris and the north celestial pole. The other two stars in the bowl—the two closer to the handle—form another set of pointer stars. To use these two, draw an imaginary line through them, and extend it in the opposite direction to the line that runs from the Pointers toward Polaris. Thus the Pointers' line aims at the north celestial pole, but the line through the other two stars of the bowl points in a nearly opposite direction, away from the celestial pole. If we extend this line by five to six times the distance between the two stars, we reach the bright star Regulus, at the base of Leo, the Lion.

LEO THE LION

Leo is a large, sprawling, elegant constellation, divided into a lion's head and hindquarters, with almost nothing visible between them. The crouching lion rests his forepaws on Regulus, with his massive head taking the form of a sickle-shaped group of stars that spreads northward from Regulus toward the celestial pole. Trailing behind the lion's foreparts, a starry triangle marks out the lion's hindquarters. This elongated triangle terminates in the star farthest from the lion's head, called Denebola, the second-brightest star in the lion. The other two stars of the hindquarters triangle form an almost perfect line with the line joining the two Pointers in the Big Dipper, if we extend that line in the direction opposite to that used to find the North Star. Regulus, whose name means "the little king," is one of the relatively few stars (Polaris is another) with a Latin name; most stars, in contrast, still carry Arabic names, or interesting mutations of these, as is true for Denebola, which derives from the Arabic word "deneb," meaning "the tail."

Although this alignment among the stars in Leo and the Big Dipper never fails, observers on summer and fall evenings will fail to discover Leo with this method, because the Lion conceals himself below the horizon. While you wait after sunset for the Lion to rise—a wait that requires many hours in late summer-

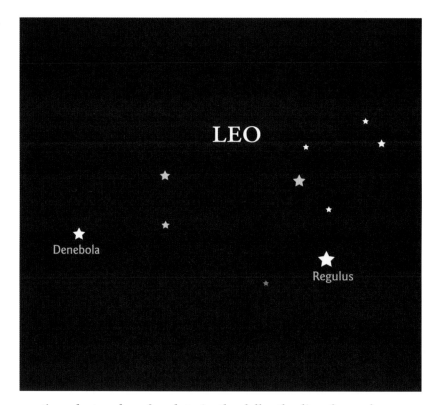

time, but only a few late in the fall—the line from the Dipper's second set of pointers, the ones closest to the Dipper's handle, will continue to point the way toward Leo, and will therefore show you its distance below the horizon.

In compensation for the Lion's absence from the night sky during the middle parts of the year, the third set of pointer stars in the Big Dipper will lead you to some of the chief constellations of spring and summer. These pointers are the three stars of the Dipper's handle, which form a short arc. The curve of this arc, extended for about four times the length of the arc, takes you to Arcturus, the brightest star in Bootes, the Herdsman. Generations of star-watchers have learned the mnemonic, "arc over to Arcturus," which remains as true today as it was centuries ago. Like Regulus, Arcturus ranks among the twenty brightest stars in the sky, which astronomers, using a nomenclature familiar to their ancient Babylonian and Greek forebears, still call "first-magnitude stars." In comparison, six of the seven stars of the Big Dipper, like Polaris and Kochab in the Little Dipper, are second-magnitude stars, which total about fifty all around the sky. Arcturus, one of the few stars to be mentioned in the Bible, appears twice in the Book of Job, once when the Lord answers Job out of the whirlwind, asking him, "Cans't thou guide Arcturus with his sons?"

Except for Sirius, which dominates the stars of winter, and Canopus and Alpha Centauri, which lie so

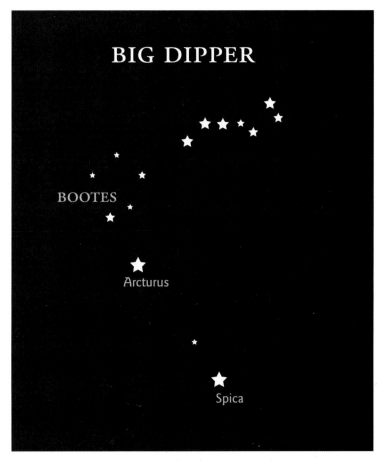

The curve of the Big Dipper's handle defines the path that allows observers to "arc over to Arcturus" and then to "speed on to Spica."

far toward the south celestial pole that they are seen only rarely from the northern hemisphere, Arcturus is the brightest star in our skies. The stars close to it form the constellation Bootes, sprawling northward from Arcturus toward the Big Dipper and Polaris. But all of Bootes's stars except for Arcturus are faint, noticeably dimmer than those in the Big Dipper, so that they can barely be seen under city conditions. Under truly dark skies, these stars become readily visible, and you can recognize, with considerable help from your imagination, the torso of a human with Arcturus at his belt.

VIRGO THE VIRGIN

In most circumstances, however, you will do best simply to follow the curve of the Dipper's handle right through Arcturus, continuing for a distance about equal to that which led you to it, to find yourself close to Spica, the brightest star in Virgo the Virgin. In astronomy lore, just as you "arc to Arcturus," so too you "speed on to Spica," passing Arcturus to reach the next truly bright star in the sky. Like Arcturus, Spica is a first-magnitude star, despite being seven times farther from us, 250 light years in comparison with Arcturus's thirty-five. Spica owes its brightness to its enormous energy output, which in turn arises from its large mass, about ten times the mass of the sun, and twenty times the mass of an average star in the Milky Way. The gravitational forces that arise from its greater mass squeeze Spica more tightly than the average star, producing a higher-than-average temperature at its center. The higher temperature in turn induces a greater rate of nuclear fusion, and we see the result glowing in Virgo. Arcturus, in contrast to Spica, has already passed its prime of life, and has become a red-giant star, still capable of producing large amounts of energy but about to enter the final phases of its stellar lifetime.

Virgo is one of the largest constellations, larger even than the Big Dipper or Leo, but it resembles Bootes in its general formlessness. Virgo represents a maiden reclining, with most of her upper body between Spica and Denebola, the star at the tip of the Lion's hindquarters. It takes an expert in conceptualization, though, to conceive a maiden, or anything else with a definite shape, in the mass of not-so-bright stars in this region. The brightest star between Spica and Denebola, Zarijan, is the second-brightest star in Virgo, but does not qualify as even a second-magnitude star.

But Virgo is not without her charms. To astronomers, the most important fact about the constellation consists of the immense number of bright galaxies that dot the sky between Spica and Leo. Thousands of individual galaxies, each comparable to our own Milky Way and containing many billion stars, form the "Virgo Cluster" of galaxies. Most of these galaxies have distances of 20 to 40 million light years from the Milky Way, roughly a million times the distance to Arcturus, or a hundred thousand times the distance to Spica. The Virgo Cluster actually spreads far outside its most densely populated region, the part that lies within the constellation Virgo; when astronomers add in its outlying regions, they define the "Virgo Supercluster," which includes our Milky Way! Thus, gazing at Virgo amounts to a look at the center of our local neighborhood—if we mean by this term the enormous cluster of galaxies, many tens of millions of light years across, that constitutes by far the closest galaxy supercluster, the one to which we belong.

TELLING TIME BY THE BIG DIPPER

As the Earth rotates, the Big Dipper faithfully reflects its motion, seeming to turn around the single stillness of the sky that we see, the point that lies directly above the North Pole of our planet. Only this point in the sky, and the complementary one above the south pole that cannot be seen from northern latitudes, maintains a constant position as the Earth rotates. All other objects in the sky appear to move from east to west, on larger or smaller circles of motion whose sizes depend on the objects' distances from the north pole in the sky, which astronomers call the north celestial pole.

Because the seven stars of the Big Dipper lie relatively close to the north pole of the sky, these stars never dip below the horizon. Instead, they perform a complete circle every day and night, though of course the stars become invisible during the daylight hours. On every clear night, the Big Dipper provides us with a celestial clock, easy to read once we understand three fundamental facts that arise from our planet's rotation on its axis and its revolution around the sun.

First, the Big Dipper furnishes us with a twenty-four-hour clock, not a twelve-hour version of the sort that has become familiar to us. This arises naturally from the fact that the Earth rotates, and the Dipper circles the pole, not in twelve but in twenty-four hours. Second, the clock turns counter-clockwise, because the

Earth's rotation makes stars circle the north celestial pole in this direction. Third, the Earth actually takes four minutes *less* than twenty-four hours, or twenty-three hours and fifty-six minutes, to perform one complete rotation with respect to the stars. If that is so, you may well ask, why do we put exactly twenty-four hours into a single day? Not because we have rounded twenty-three hours and fifty-six minutes up to twenty-four hours, but because we keep time on Earth with respect to the *sun*, not the stars.

Picture the Earth's two basic motions, its daily rotation and its yearly orbit around the sun. Imagine yourself on a journey outward from the Earth's North Pole that carries you to a position in space far above the solar system, so that you can look down on the Earth's counterclockwise rotation and its equally counterclockwise motion in orbit. Then you can see that even after the Earth has completed a single complete rotation with respect to the stars, it must rotate a bit more in order to regain its original orientation with respect to the sun because it has moved a bit along its orbit. Every day, the Earth covers approximately $\frac{1}{365}$ of its complete yearly orbit. As a result, when the Earth has regained its original position with respect to the stars after its daily rotation, it still must complete an additional $\frac{1}{365}$ more of a rotation, which takes $\frac{1}{365}$ of a day, or four minutes, in order to regain its original orientation with respect to the sun. Because we keep solar time, our clocks show that the stars rise above the horizon, or regain a particular orientation with respect to the horizon, four minutes earlier on each successive evening.

The combination of daily rotation and yearly orbital motion thus carry the stars through a changing cycle of appearance, until the passage of a full year restores them to the same positions in the sky at the same time of night that they had one year earlier. This implies that we can employ the Big Dipper as a clock by keeping track of the calendar and by observing the position of the Dipper with respect to Polaris, the North Star.

Take a close look at the Big Dipper and the Pointers that show the way to Polaris, the North Star. Then conceive Polaris to be the center of a clock face, and imagine the line from the two Pointers in the Big Dipper's bowl as the hand of the clock. At 4 A.M. on January 1, this line will rise straight above Polaris: the Big Dipper, much higher in the sky than the North Star, then lies nearly overhead, and the line from

Polaris to the Pointers rises upwards from the north point on the horizon. Twelve hours later, even though daylight obscures the stars, we know that the Pointers will be directly underneath Polaris, close to or even slightly below the horizon, because the Earth will have made one-half of a complete rotation on its axis.

As the year passes, however, the Earth moves around the sun, and the objects that we see in the sky will typically regain their positions four minutes earlier on each successive night. A month's worth of these four-minute intervals adds up to two hours, so by February 1, we need wait only until 2 A.M. for the Pointers to stand directly over the North Star, and our imaginary clock hand will rise straight up from the North Star. On March 1, this alignment will occur at midnight; on April 1, it will happen at 10 P.M.; and so throughout the year, with the line-up appearing two hours earlier each month, until the next January 1 will once again see the clock hand straight up at 4 A.M.

Thus the Earth's motions, which govern the nightly appearance of the stars, furnish us with the rule for using the Big Dipper as a timepiece on any day of the year. Locate the two pointer stars, Dubhe and Merak, at the end of the Dipper's bowl, and use them to find

the North Star, Polaris. With Polaris as the clock center, imagine the hand of the clock to extend outwards from Polaris to the Pointers. This line furnishes the hour hand of a twenty-four-hour clock, with midnight at the top of its face and noon at the bottom. You must remember, however, that this clock runs backwards—that is, counterclockwise—so that 6 A.M. lies at the midpoint of the left-hand side of the clock face, and 6 P.M. appears at the midpoint of the right-hand side. Bearing this in mind, simply look for the hour on the clock indicated by the imaginary hand, the line from Polaris to the Pointers. This hour will be the actual time on March 1, but on all other days of the year, we must adjust our clock for the Earth's changing position in its orbit by subtracting from the clock time an amount (which may be negative) equal to:

(2 hours x number of months past January 1) – 4 hours

Thus on March 15, we subtract 1 hour, because we are 2.5 months past January 1; on June 15, we subtract 7 hours; and on September 7, we subtract 12.5 hours from the time that the Dipper's clock hand seems to show us. During the two months before

March 1, we subtract a negative amount, which means we add a positive number, in computing the amount described above. On January 15, for example, we would add 3 hours, and on February 15, 1 hour to the time that the Dipper clock shows.

Using the Big Dipper as a clock ties us into the seasonal changes in the appearance of the heavens, which arise from the Earth's stately progression around the sun, year after year, following the laws that Isaac Newton first explained. As Albert Einstein wrote in admiration of Newton during a visit to Cambridge University (I have translated from his more rollicking German):

> *Gaze upon the stars that teach us*
> *How the master's thoughts can reach us:*
> *Each one follows Newton's math*
> *Silently along its path.*

MEDITATION: HUMAN TIME AND DEEP TIME

Of all the constellations, the Big Dipper calls to us most directly. Its easily recognizable shape, seven stars arranged in a bowl and a handle, speaks to us of a simpler time when everyone used a dipper or a drinking gourd. This shape also carries a hidden meaning, one that speaks of time intervals so long that human imagination has difficulty conceiving them.

Before turning to this deep subject, note that the *distances* to the seven stars of the Big Dipper mark epochs familiar to us from our relatively recent history, since the stars lie at distances between 77 and 227 light years. In astronomical terms, the time that the light from these stars has traveled to reach us amounts to a single instant. Far greater amounts of time must pass before an observer would see any change in the Big Dipper, which has the same shape today that it had when Columbus sailed the seas, when slaves built the pyramids in Egypt, and when our ancestors first invented agriculture. But when we conceive still greater spans of time, we can truly recognize that the *positions* of the seven stars on the sky will happen to form a dipper only for a snapshot in cosmic time.

We have seen that the Earth's rotation axis performs a slow wobble, tracing out a circular path on the sky that takes 26,000 years to return to its starting point. This motion, however, is an entirely local one: the Earth slowly changes the direction toward which its rotation axis points in space. The stars continue on their majestic ways, grouped into their familiar constellations, and all that happens as the result of the wobbling axis is that the north and south celestial poles wander in a circular motion among the constellations. The last full cycle of 26,000 years includes the entire history of human civilization on Earth, including all the prehistory only dimly glimpsed through archaeological research. A great debate continues among historical anthropologists as to whether the first humans to reach the Americas arrived about halfway back through such a cycle—that is, about 13,000 years ago—or at least a full cycle ago. And even a full cycle of 26,000 years will not produce much change in the shape of the Big Dipper.

But if we think ourselves still deeper into the past, we will see that the passage of not tens but hundreds of thousands of years will give the Big Dipper a noticeably new configuration, and a million years will destroy it as a dipper. Instead, a million years from now, as a million years ago, the stars will have quite a different set of positions with respect to one another. The name "Big Dipper" may remain to confuse our descendants, and the stars themselves will shine for many millions of years, but the shape will ooze itself slowly from the familiar dipper into nothing we can recognize as familiar.

What will produce these changes? The stars in their courses are in actual motion, not simply seeming to move across the sky as the Earth spins. Every star in our Milky Way galaxy has its own orbit around the galactic center, an orbit in which the star balances its tendency to fly off into space against the combined gravitational pull from all the other stars. As a result of this balance, stars like our sun move in nearly circular paths around the center of the Milky Way, nowhere near this violent heart of the galaxy, but still gravitationally bound into the galactic web of stars. These orbits may be similar, carrying each star in basically the same direction around the center, but are never identical: each star has its own average distance from the galactic center, and its own deviation from perfect circularity in its orbit. Each of the galaxy's stars wheels in a slow, intricate ballet that carries any two stars sometimes closer, sometimes farther from one another.

So look at the seven stars of the Big Dipper. Picture them in their starry courses, endlessly circling the Milky Way, taking about two hundred and fifty million years to do so. Then imagine our sun as well, moving on a similar orbit, likewise in nearly circular motion around the galaxy. Twenty complete trips has the sun made, more or less, since it came into being with its planets, nearly five billion years ago. The Big Dipper's stars, younger than our sun, have completed fewer orbits, but like the sun, they are as always on their way around another one. Carried on our own galactic orbit by the star that gravitationally owns and controls us, we look across the light years to seven other stars that move along seven slightly different trajectories. If every day and night lasted not twenty-four hours but a thousand years, we would see the Big Dipper distort within a few hundred of these days, to the point that its dipperness would disappear completely within a single "year." In this model of cosmic time, the sun was born five million "days" ago. Only during the past "year," more or less, did the Big Dipper take shape, and it will be gone after a single such "year" has elapsed.

Enjoy it while you can!

Chapter *Five*

Three Stars That Belong to You

This wide-angle view shows Orion (left center), Sirius (far left), and Comet Hale-Bopp (right center), with the Hyades and Pleiades between Orion and the comet.

To find the Big Dipper is an easy task when you look toward the north on a clear dark night. Indeed, locating the Big Dipper is such a piece of cake that most people are content to let this feat represent the alpha and omega of their star knowledge. Unknown to this majority, but familiar to those who love the heavens, a constellation easily visible in the skies of late fall and winter offers a group of stars as recognizable as those in the Big Dipper and far more stunning, one that also provides the key to finding all the significant stars of the colder months. This constellation, Orion the Hunter, embraces a vivid array of bright stars that actually seem to form the outline of a giant in the sky—a rare example of cosmic reality imitating human invention.

To find Orion, you need only look for "three stars that belong to you." I take this phrase from Spike Milligan, the British entertainer best known for his long-time collaboration with Peter Sellers on the radio comedy "The Goon Show." In recalling his boyhood in India, where he felt isolated from most of the world, Milligan told how he looked to the stars for comfort.

He soon came to recognize, night after night, a close-packed triplet, three bright stars in a line that rose high overhead, and decided that those were *his* stars, the three that he called his own. This sweet story encapsulates the captivating power of stargazing.

To an astronomer, Milligan's stars are instantaneously recognizable from his words alone. They are the three stars that form the belt of Orion the Hunter, which ranks high among the largest, finest, and most interesting constellations in the skies. Once you find Orion, you will forever have a companion on clear, dark winter nights, capable of guiding you over the crackling and frozen terrain, or showing you splendors of the sky only dimly imagined before you acquired this connection with the cosmos.

Activity One:
Finding Orion the Hunter

Finding the Hunter on a clear night in winter or spring poses an easy task, thanks to the three stars in Orion's belt—the only three bright stars that appear so close together, evenly spaced and almost equal to one another in brightness. The three stars in Orion's belt rise in a vertical line above the eastern horizon in late fall and early winter. Still later in the season, as the new year runs toward February, Orion will have already risen well above the horizon by the time that night falls; even later, as spring draws near, you will find the Hunter directly above the southern horizon. In early spring, darkness finds Orion toward the west, ready to sink below the horizon for another season of slumber. From the harvest season to apple-blossom time, you can easily catch the Hunter by his belt, and make these three stars your own.

For example, if you turn your face toward the east at about 9 P.M. early in December, you will find Orion's belt close to the horizon, but already well above it. For dates earlier in the year, you must add two hours per month to this time, since that is the time change that the Earth's motion around the sun imposes on the rising and setting of the stars. Thus, for example, if you want to see Orion in late October, you must wait until midnight to see his belt well-risen above the horizon. A full year brings you back to your starting point by telling you to look twenty-four hours earlier, that is, at the same time of night.

To be sure that you have found Orion, ask yourself, "Are these stars the only example of a fine, close threesome in the sky? Could I have mistaken three other stars for the belt of Orion?" Almost certainly you have not, but to eliminate all doubt, you should search out the other bright stars in Orion, which will verify that you have indeed found the Hunter. Look to either side of Orion's belt, and you will find two stars even brighter than the three stars in the belt. One of these is Betelgeuse, the bright star in the Hunter's shoulder, which lies to the left (northward) of the belt as Orion rises; the other is Rigel, the bright star in the Hunter's foot, to the right (southward) of the belt. The distance on the sky from each of these stars to Orion's belt is about 2.5 times the length of the belt itself.

Once you have found Orion, pause to congratulate yourself. Many may talk airily about this task, but relatively few accomplish it. When I first became interested in astronomy, twelve years old and ready for just about anything, I read about Orion during the early fall, as the school year started, and wondered why I had never noticed this fine set of stars in contemplating the sky. I was not in the habit of staying up until or past midnight, so I could only dream and wait—until the evening when I joined my classmates on our junior-high-school night out. Walking home with a couple of friends that evening, exulting in our new-found freedom to stay up so late on a Friday night, talking of anything but astronomy, I happened to look toward the east, and there was Orion, just as described in books but far more beautiful. When I directed the attention of my twelve-year-old companions to the constellation, they showed me new regard, the respect that astronomers have always gained from the public. This feeling can also be yours.

Five stars make Orion immediately recognizable, the three in his belt plus still brighter Betelgeuse and Rigel on either side. Take a moment to examine the colors of the three stars in the belt and of the two even brighter stars on either side. Unless the cosmos or your eyes are playing a trick on you, you will immediately see that Betelgeuse, to the north of the belt, shines with a noticeably orange hue, while Rigel, to the south, glows with a steely, blue-white light. The stars in the belt have blue-white colors that match Rigel's, without a touch of red or orange. These stars' different colors arise from tremendous physical differences among them.

Betelgeuse has expanded to become a red super-giant star, and in doing so has lowered its temperature, so that it glows with a ruddy hue. Rigel has a surface temperature more than ten times that of Betelgeuse, giving it a steel-blue color. The three stars in Orion's belt are even hotter and therefore even bluer than Rigel.

Two more stars complete the body of Orion the Hunter. One of them, Bellatrix, furnishes Orion with his dimmer shoulder, not so bright as Betelgeuse, but still a notably bright star that slightly outshines each of the stars in the belt. As Orion rises, you will find Bellatrix above and to the right of Betelgeuse, a bit closer than Betelgeuse to the three stars in the belt and a bit higher in the sky than the belt itself. The other star to note, Saiph, forms Orion's second foot, but definitely plays second fiddle to Rigel. A line from Betelgeuse to Rigel, from the Hunter's bright shoulder to his bright foot, passes through the middle of his belt, and so does a line from his faint shoulder to his faint foot. The only flaw in this majestic plan consists of Saiph's relative faintness; of the seven key stars in Orion, Saiph is the one that you must exert some extra effort to find.

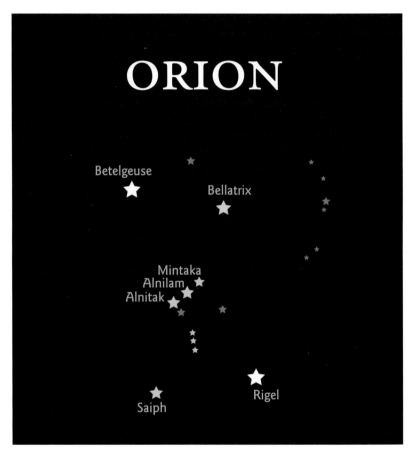

This diagram presents the bright stars of the constellation Orion the Hunter, easily recognizable by the three bright stars that form Orion's belt, with still brighter stars in the Hunter's bright foot and shoulder.

Activity Two:
The Jewel in the Sword

Seven bright stars—three in his belt, two in his shoulders, and two in his feet—delineate Orion the Hunter. If all the constellations provided such excellent representations of their eponymous heroes and heroines, then star spotting would be far simpler, and more of us would spend fine hours admiring the patterns that the heavens spread before us on every clear night. In reality, Orion and the Big Dipper mark the pinnacle of human success in joining our legends to the stars. We must take the stars as we find them, and in Orion we find them fine indeed, so excellent in suggesting the outline of a man that we can forgive Orion's lack of a visible head. The host of relatively faint stars that spread westward from Betelgeuse and Bellatrix, in the direction away from the belt, are usually taken to represent the Hunter's cloak, which he has flung majestically above his shoulder, perhaps to keep the cloak between himself and Taurus the Bull.

But as if in compensation for having no visible head, Orion possesses a mighty sword, whose central jewel shines not with a single star's light but rather with the glow from a newborn cluster of stars. If you seek to share astronomers' feelings of wonder at what Orion hath wrought, take a moment to admire the jewel in his sword, which astronomers call the Orion Nebula.

Find the three stars in Orion's belt, and examine the area between the belt and Orion's two feet, bright Rigel and fainter Saiph. You should easily see the three stars that form Orion's sword, not so bright as the three stars in the belt but still easily visible, shining nearly as brightly as Saiph does. The three stars in Orion's sword, spaced twice as closely as those in the belt, form a line extending away from the belt. If you extend this line in your imagination, you will find that it almost bisects the line between Rigel and Saiph. Extended in the opposite direction, the line of the sword almost precisely meets Alnilam, the middle star in Orion's belt.

It is Orion's sword that makes the Hunter complete, and in his sword we find the reason that astronomers who discuss Orion usually refer not to the constellation in general but to this specific jewel of light and its immediate surroundings. In these mysteries, concentrate your gaze on the central star of the three that form Orion's sword. On a good clear night, you can see even without binoculars that this star appears to be fuzzy, shining with light not so concentrated as that from the stars that mark Orion's extremities. A pair of binoculars will remove all doubt, and will reveal that here at the center of Orion's sword lies a diffuse mass of gas, lit from within. If your binoculars and the darkness of night are sufficiently fine, you can see some of the stars that lie enveloped within this gas and illuminate their surroundings. This is the Orion Nebula, the closest large star-forming region in our Milky Way galaxy.

The Orion Nebula plays a central role in astronomers' attempts to understand the mysteries of how stars form, and why stars are born with the range of sizes, masses, and luminosities that astronomers have now uncovered. This mass of gas, dust, and stars shines with the light produced by dozens of young, hot, highly luminous stars, all of which formed within the past million years, and none of which will last longer than a few million years before burning itself out. Close though it may be among all the star-forming regions in our Milky Way galaxy, the Orion Nebula nevertheless lies as far from us as any individual star that we can easily see with our unaided eyes. The light from the jewel in the sword has traveled for 1,500 years to reach us—even farther than the distance to Rigel and the stars in Orion's belt, which, at 1,300 light years of distance, rank among the most distant bright stars in our skies, and have nearly two hundred times the distance to Sirius, the brightest of all the stars we can see. Sirius owes its brilliance to the happenstance of being a relatively close neighbor, and a journey from the sun to Sirius would barely begin to qualify as a significant trip through the Milky Way. In Orion, however, we can look outward to distances that span a significant fraction, though a small one, of the total distance across our galaxy. We inhabit a relatively obscure suburb of the Milky Way galaxy, whose center lies 25,000 light years away, in the direction almost opposite to that in which we see Orion. When we admire the Orion Nebula, we are looking outward from the center of our galaxy. This distance marks the edge of our visible universe, until we use binoculars or a telescope to assist our view. (The great exception to this statement, the Andromeda galaxy, is described in chapter 9.)

THE HUNTER AND THE SCORPION

For those who love the lore of the stars, it comes as no accident that Orion marks out the direction opposite to the Milky Way's center. Our galaxy's center appears in the constellation Sagittarius, close to its boundary with the constellation Scorpius (see page 117). Like Orion, Scorpius (the Scorpion) is easy to recognize, because it too is one of the few constellations that actually resembles the object whose name it carries. Scorpius has a fine curved tail that gives it easy identification, and in legend carried the sting that killed Orion. To assure celestial harmony, legends tell us, the Hunter and the Scorpion occupy opposite points on the sky, so that they can never be seen at the same time. Instead, Orion dominates the skies from late fall to early spring, whereas Scorpius can be seen from late spring through early fall.

The Orion Nebula offers astronomers the chance to see star formation in action. To be sure, this "action" proceeds too slowly to produce significant changes on human time scales, but it embraces complete transfigurations on astronomical ones. During the span of a few million years, less than one one-thousandth of the present age of the sun and the Earth, the Orion Nebula has converted and will convert interstellar gas and dust into stars, of which the brightest will "soon" be gone, while the more modest, sunlike ones, invisible without an excellent telescope, will endure for billions of years. The small spot of light at the center of Orion's sword shows us cosmic evolution at its most visible, slow but effective.

That small spot of light, however, represents the tip of an iceberg: *all* of Orion is turning itself into stars! That statement contains a small exaggeration, but only because some of the matter has *already* become stars that shine. Observations made with radio waves and infrared radiation, which can show us gas and dust too cold to radiate visible light, have now revealed to astronomers what no one suspected when only visible light painted our cosmic pictures. In galactic terms, the Orion Nebula represents a small, bright blister on a vast interstellar cloud that spreads all through Orion and extends into neighboring constellations as well. We see, in effect, only the near side of this immense cloud, and in visible light we see only the Orion Nebula plus a few of the other stars that have recently formed: Rigel, Saiph, Alnilam, Alnitak, Mintaka, and the stars next to the Orion Nebula in Orion's sword. All of these stars lie about 1,300 light years away, a bit less than the distance to the Orion Nebula; they have apparently all formed within the past few million years, and they testify (along with the observations made by radio and infrared astronomers) to the vast numbers of stars—several millions by the best estimates—that are waiting to be born in the dark, cold recesses of the great interstellar cloud in Orion.

Activity Three:
The Great Constellations of Winter

As befits a mighty hunter waking from deep sleep, Orion rises above the eastern horizon in a horizontal posture, with his belt nearly upright, his shoulders toward the north, and his feet toward the south. As the Hunter rises, however, he gradually loses his supine posture, until finally, as he sinks below the western horizon, he stands completely upright. Observers on the western shores of the United States can watch Orion sink into the sea, with Rigel and Saiph disappearing first, followed by the Hunter's sword, then his belt, his shoulders, and finally his cloak.

Through his swing across the sky, Orion occupies the center of the finest group of bright stars and con- stellations visible to observers in the northern hemisphere. Of the twenty brightest stars in the sky, which astronomers have called "first-magnitude stars" for two thousand years, two appear in Orion (Rigel and Betelgeuse) and two more in the hunting dogs that follow Orion through the heavens (Sirius and Procyon, in the Big Dog and the Little Dog, respectively). One of the first-magnitude stars precedes the Hunter (Aldebaran, in Taurus the Bull), one lies in the Twins to the north (Pollux, whose near-twin Castor falls just short of qualifying for the top twenty), and one more, Capella, appears in Orion's neighbor to the north, Auriga the Charioteer. Thus, seven of the twenty first-magnitude stars in the sky can be found within just one-tenth of the full vault of heaven, the imaginary celestial sphere that circles the Earth. Thanks to the skymarks that Orion offers, it is a duck-soup contest to find and identify these bright stars and their home constellations.

TAURUS THE BULL

Once again, Orion's belt provides the natural starting point for a tour of the heavens. Start by extending the imaginary line passing through the three stars of the belt outward in both directions. If you extend the line toward the west—upwards from the belt whenever Orion is near the eastern horizon—you will pass close to the bright star Aldebaran (accent on the second syllable), the brightest star in Taurus the Bull. Aldebaran's orange color bespeaks the fact that, like Betelgeuse, this star has become a "red giant," an aging, swollen star, puffing its outer layers to an ever-greater size.

Aldebaran lies at one tip of a V-shaped arrangement of much fainter stars, which nevertheless can be seen clearly on a dark night. The V opens toward the northwest, which means that the imaginary line across the top of the V runs parallel to Orion's belt. This V of stars provides Taurus with his horns, and in fact the proud Bull shows nothing but his horns, along with a few modest stars in his forequarters, to the unaided eye. But we should not pass lightly by the horns of the Bull. Except for Aldebaran, the V of stars consists of the brightest stars in the Hyades star cluster, a group of several hundred stars about 150 light years from the solar system. The Hyades are in fact the closest star cluster to us, and astronomers have studied their colors and motions for many years, seeking to unravel the mysteries of how stars are born and evolve.

THE PLEIADES

By pure chance, the second-closest star cluster, even more eye-catching than the Hyades, lies in almost the same direction as the Hyades. These stars can be found by continuing to extend the line from Orion's belt to Aldebaran, passing by Aldebaran and the Hyades, and then continuing for a stretch of distance about equal to that which brought you from the belt to Aldebaran. There lie the Pleiades, a small dipper of stars, glistening in the darkness with the light from—how many stars? Can you see four? You are in the city, and perhaps need to have your vision checked. Six? Then your eyes are good, and you have a fine dark sky in which to view the heavens. Seven? Your vision rates better than excellent, and you have almost certainly left city lights behind. Eight, nine, or ten? You may be dreaming—or have you taken a pair of binoculars to assist your gaze? In that case, you should see dozens of stars, the brightest of the three hundred or so that comprise the Pleiades star cluster. The fact that the Pleiades lie more than three times farther from us than the Hyades, five hundred light years to 150, make them appear to us in a more compact form; in absolute terms, both star clusters span about ten light years in diameter. The Pleiades, called the Seven Sisters, the Seven Virgins, or the Seven Doves by various ancient astronomers, rank among the most identifiable sets of stars, and have captivated many a culture in marking out the heavens. The ancient Greeks saw the Pleiades as six stars plus one that had disappeared, supposedly from sorrow over the fall of Troy. Aldebaran, which in fact means "the follower" in Arabic, refers to the fact that Aldebaran follows the Pleiades through the sky as the Earth turns, just as Orion follows Aldebaran and the Big Dog follows him.

This photograph shows Orion mostly sunk below the horizon, with Gemini directly above. Castor and Pollux appear near the top of the photograph.

CANIS MAJOR, THE BIG DOG

To find the Big Dog, look along the line of Orion's belt in the direction opposite to the one that points to Aldebaran, the Hyades, and the Pleiades. There shines Sirius, the Dog Star, brightest of all the stars in the sky. No one who extends the line of Orion's belt toward the east can miss the glare of the Dog Star, provided that you give Sirius time to rise, an hour or so after the last of the three stars in Orion's belt has cleared the horizon. Sirius forms the eye of Canis Major, the Big Dog. If you look along the same line of the belt but still farther from Orion than Sirius, you will see four or five fairly bright stars that form the Big Dog's hind legs and hindquarters. Closer to Sirius, in the direction perpendicular to the line from the belt to the Dog Star, you can see the second brightest star in the constellation, Murzim, which marks the tip of the dog's muzzle; on the opposite side of Sirius to Murzim, and at the same distance from Sirius as Murzim, you will find Muliphein, which marks the Big Dog's ear. In a good mood, you can picture Canis Major as Snoopy, dancing his way behind Orion, with his head not turned upward to gaze at the Hunter but instead aligned toward the dim stars below (southward of) Orion. This is an appropriate posture for a dog, since these dim stars, in the direction toward which Orion's sword points, form the constellation of Lepus the Hare.

CANIS MINOR, THE LITTLE DOG

Canis Major offers nothing so satisfying as Orion in the way of justifying his name with his starry configuration. Nevertheless, in this regard the Big Dog far outdoes both Lepus the Hare and Canis Minor, the Little Dog. The Little Dog consists, for naked-eye astronomy, of just two stars! By far the brighter of these, Procyon, forms one corner of a large, nearly perfect equilateral triangle, of which the other two corners are occupied by Sirius and by Betelgeuse, the brighter of Orion's two shoulders. Astronomers often call this the "Winter Triangle," since it appears to greatest advantage during the winter months, and nicely complements the even better "Summer Triangle" that dominates the skies of summer (see page 131). Close by Procyon, whose name means "before the dog" in Greek and refers to the fact that the Little Dog rises before the Big One does, you can see the Little Dog's much fainter second star, whose Arabic name (known to experts only) is Gomeisa.

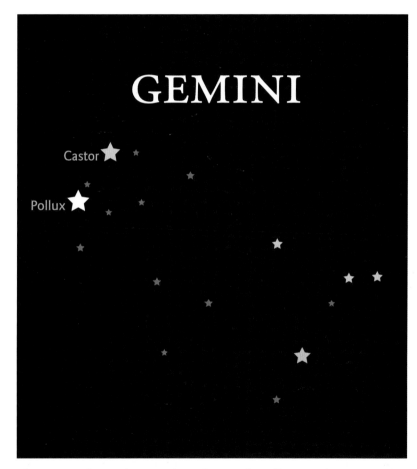

The stars in Gemini form two lines that run from Castor and Pollux, the heads of the Twins, toward the constellation Orion.

GEMINI, THE TWINS, AND AURIGA, THE CHARIOTEER

Now that you have used Orion's belt to find Aldebaran, the Hyades, the Pleiades, and Sirius, you can employ the Hunter's other parts to locate the constellations Gemini and Auriga. To find Gemini, extend a line all the way through Orion, from Rigel in his bright foot through Betelgeuse in his bright shoulder, for the same distance as that separating these two stars; you will then find yourself in the lower parts of Gemini the Twins. Gemini consists of two parallel lines of medium-bright stars that each terminate in the two brightest stars, Castor and Pollux, which mark the heads of the twins. Of these two stars, Pollux shines with redder light than Castor does, and is lower in the sky during the hours after Gemini rises in the east. If you recall your use of Orion's belt to find Aldebaran and Sirius, you can see that Pollux lies on the side of Gemini toward Sirius, while Castor is on the side toward Aldebaran. Pollux is a red giant like Aldebaran, but Castor is neither a red giant nor a single star; instead, it is one of the most complex star systems known, in which six individual stars move in orbit!

A CELESTIAL DANCE

In Castor, pairs of stars are performing rapid dances (as star motions go) around their common centers of mass, and as they do so, the three separate pairs are performing a much slower, larger balletic movement around the center of mass of the entire system. All this astronomers know from studying Castor with great telescopes and spectroscopes; for the unaided observer, Castor looks like any other star.

The seventh of the first-magnitude stars of the winter sky can be found by using Orion's sword as a guideline. Just take the line of the sword and extend it upwards, passing through the center of Orion's belt, continue through a point between the Hunter's shoulders, and proceed onward for a distance equal to nearly twice the distance from Betelgeuse to Rigel. There you will see Capella, the head of Auriga the Charioteer. In sober truth, Auriga looks more like a deflated pentagon than a race-course driver. The Latin name Capella means "the little she-goat," but neither the star nor its constellation drew much attention from ancient Greek and Latin astronomers, since Auriga does not lie in the zodiac or play an important calendrical role. In contrast, ancient Egyptians had paid great honor to Capella, assigning it the place of honor in their worship of the great god Ptah, and ancient Indian astronomers named the star "Brahma Ridaya," the Heart of Brahma. Star lore has its fickle side.

There you have them: Orion and its neighbor constellations, the Bull, the Big Dog, the Little Dog, the Twins, and the Charioteer. In star terms, the three in Orion's belt are flanked by Betelgeuse and Bellatrix to the north, Rigel and Saiph to the south, with Orion's sword hanging southward from his belt. Aldebaran lies along the belt's westward extension, with the Hyades nearby and the Pleiades still farther along the line; Sirius lies in the other direction, where the belt points eastward. Castor and Pollux appear at the end of the long imaginary line that runs from Rigel through Betelgeuse, and Procyon lies below them, forming an equilateral triangle with Sirius and Betelgeuse. Finally, Capella lies due north of Orion, in the direction that Orion's sword marks out by pointing through the middle of the Hunter's belt. Savor these stars well; you shall not find their like elsewhere on the sky—until and unless you travel to the southern hemisphere, and see the Southern Cross gleaming next to Alpha and Beta Centauri (page 174).

THE OTHER HALF OF THE SKY

We have seen that Orion contains two of the twenty brightest stars in the sky, and that the brightest of all these twenty, Sirius the Dog Star, lies not far to the southeast, in the head of Orion's Big Dog. By an interesting application of chance, the second-brightest of all stars, called Canopus (accent on the second syllable), lies relatively close to Sirius on the sky. Yet Canopus remains almost unseen by most of the population in Europe and the United States, and receives little recognition from those who do happen to see the star.

What gives Canopus the works, so far as fame is concerned? The astronomical answer turns out to be simple, once we recognize that we live on a nearly spherical planet. Canopus lies far to the south on the celestial sphere, at a point just over halfway from the celestial equator, the imaginary circle on the sky halfway between the north and south celestial poles, to the south celestial pole. Sirius itself has a position well to the south of the celestial equator, and for that reason does not rise so far above the southern horizon as do the stars in Orion, Gemini, or Taurus, or Procyon, the star that forms the heart of the Little Dog. But Sirius lies only about 18 degrees to the south of the celestial equator, just one-fifth of the 90 degrees that separate the celestial equator from the south celestial pole. Canopus is almost directly south of Sirius on the celestial sphere, about 35 degrees away from it—a distance on the sky a little greater than the distance from Sirius to Betelgeuse, the red star in Orion's bright shoulder. Although a glance at the sky shows that this represents a relatively modest distance around the celestial sphere, it turns out to be just enough to keep Canopus out of sight for nearly everyone in the United States. The second-brightest star in the sky lies 53 degrees to the south of the celestial equator, and 37 degrees from the south celestial pole. Who, then, can see Canopus?

The branch of sky lore called "spherical astronomy," which describes how distances and angles on the celestial sphere relate to one another and to the Earth's rotation and revolution, reveal to the initiated that an observer located on Earth north of the equator can see only part of the celestial sphere. Sooner or later, all of the celestial sphere that lies to the north of the celestial equator will rise above the observer's horizon, and so too will a portion of the other half of the celestial sphere, the half that lies to the south of the celestial equator. But part of the southern half of the celestial sphere, the portion closest to the south celestial pole, will never rise at all. This portion remains forever hidden—until and unless the observer moves closer toward the equator, thus gaining the chance to see more of this hidden part.

How far south can any particular observer see? The rule is simple: take your latitude and subtract it from 90 degrees. That specifies, in degrees, the distance to which you can see to the south of the celestial equator. An observer at 90 degrees north latitude, braving the weather at the North Pole, could see zero degrees to the south of the celestial equator. For this observer, the celestial sphere will spin and spin, always showing the same stars, the half of the celestial sphere that lies to the north of the celestial equator. Orion's belt, which lies just below the celestial equator, would circle just below the observer's horizon, forever prevented from rising by the fact that the Earth is spherical.

As it happens, few observers attempt to follow the stars from the North Pole, and fewer still succeed, owing to the weather conditions that prevail there. An observer at 45 degrees north latitude, in New Hampshire, Wisconsin, or Oregon, can see 45 degrees to the south of the celestial equator, just halfway down to the south celestial pole. This observer can easily see Sirius, but can never see Canopus. Observers in New York and Philadelphia, at 42 and 40 degrees north latitude, can see 48 and 50 degrees, respectively, to the south of the celestial equator, still not far enough to reveal Canopus at 53 degrees south. At 38 degrees north, the latitude of San Francisco and Washington, DC, Canopus just fails to clear an observer's southern horizon, because these observers can see only 52 degrees to the south of the celestial equator. If you want to see the second-brightest star, you must venture well south of 38 degrees, to a latitude of 35 degrees or less. For example, observers at 34 degrees north latitude, in Los Angeles, Albuquerque, Memphis, or Charlotte, can see a full 56 degrees to the south of the celestial equator; those in Atlanta and Dallas can see one or two degrees farther south, and those in Houston,

New Orleans, or Jacksonville, at 30 degrees north latitude, can see 70 degrees south of the equator. These observers have the chance to see Canopus, which rises to a height between 3 and 17 degrees above the southern horizon, but the opportunity must be seized with vigor, at the proper time of the year and of the night.

Consider, for example, an observer in Dallas, who can see 58 degrees below the equator. Situated 53 degrees south of the celestial equator, Canopus will rise no more than 5 degrees above the horizon, only $\frac{1}{18}$ of the way from the horizon to the zenith, as it crosses the meridian (the imaginary line that runs from the north to the south points on the horizon, passing through the point directly overhead) of this observer. Nevertheless, 5 degrees offers a good chance to see the star, provided that you have a clear view to the south and know when to look. Here, Sirius will be your guide and marker. Just follow Sirius's motion in the sky and wait for it to cross the meridian; when it does so, look directly to the south of Sirius to spot Canopus, the second-brightest of all our stars. At a latitude of 35 degrees, you can begin to see Canopus perhaps half an hour before it crosses the meridian, and can do so for about half an hour after this crossing. At a latitude of 32 degrees, you should be able to see Canopus for nearly an hour before and another hour after it reaches its high point on the meridian, 5 degrees above the southern horizon.

For those who prefer to plan well in advance, and to avoid the cold hours of waiting that may dampen the astronomical spirit, I provide a list of the times at which Canopus reaches its maximum height above the southern horizon on different days of the year. The mathematically minded will note that this time occurs two hours earlier per month, advancing like clockwork, as we described on page 75.

WHEN CANOPUS REACHES
ITS MAXIMUM HEIGHT
ABOVE THE SOUTHERN HORIZON

Date	Time
November 1	3:50 A.M.
November 15	2:50 A.M.
December 1	1:50 A.M.
December 15	12:50 A.M.
January 1	11:50 P.M.
January 15	10:50 A.M.
February 1	9:50 P.M.
February 15	8:50 P.M.
March 1	7:50 P.M.

Chapter *Six*

The World Sparkles in Light

Rainbows appear when sunlight reflects from the interiors of myriad water droplets. Sometimes a second rainbow appears outside the first one.

Nature and evolution have endowed us with five senses: taste, smell, feeling, hearing, and sight. In experiencing the world around us, we rely on all of these, processing our sensory inputs through highly developed, utterly natural computers whose RAM and ROM may become compromised with increasing age, but whose abilities are the stuff of humanity. Of the five senses, only one—touch—works by direct contact with our bodies. The other four rely on our receiving and interpreting the information that our specialized organs of taste, smell, hearing, and sight acquire for our benefit.

Three of these four, taste, smell, and hearing, record the impact of actual molecules, the bits of matter that make up the world around us. We *hear* because molecules of oxygen and nitrogen in the air, provoked into vibration by the disturbances we call sound waves, shake the membranes of our eardrums as they strike; our eardrums rattle the tiny bones connected to them, the hammer, anvil, and stirrup, which in turn stimulate nerve endings that send messages to our brains. Our sense of *taste* relies on specialized receptors on our tongues, which recognize different types of molecules, distinguishing sweet from sour and interpreting a range of flavors by relaying the results of their analysis to the brain. Similarly, we *smell* a variety of scents when our olfactory glands, which line the interiors of our noses, detect different types of molecules, and send the news through other specialized nerve fibers into the appropriate portions of the neural cortex.

WHAT IS LIGHT?

The fifth of our senses operates differently. We *see* not because solid particles impinge upon our eyes, but rather because our eyes can detect streams of massless particles called photons. In contrast to the molecules that carry the news about taste, smell, and sound, photons have no mass whatsoever, and therefore hardly qualify as particles in the usual sense of the word, whose defining characteristic resides in their solid masses. Instead, as physicists finally admitted after years of confusion, photons have the characteristics of *both* waves and particles, without qualifying purely as either one! Our eyes record the impact of these strange entities, and thereby provide us with images of the world. We can state this result more eas-ily than we can comprehend the facts that make it happen. Nevertheless, we can try.

To understand photons, we must begin by accepting the notion that a particle can exist with no mass at all. Photons have no weight, no heft, no hold-it-in-your-hand reality. Yet they certainly exist, and their best claim to recognition, in terms of how we humans understand the world, rests in the fact that every photon carries kinetic energy. Indeed, the simplest way to conceive a photon is to imagine a tiny bundle of energy, traveling at the speed of light in a straight line, sometimes individually, sometimes as part of the huge hordes of similar photons that comprise a beam of light.

Because photons have no mass, they exist only so long as they move—and rapidly at that. Photons zip through empty space at the enormous velocity of 186,000 miles per second, equal to 6 trillion miles per year, unless and until they encounter something solid—an atom, a molecule, a dust grain, or a larger assemblage of matter, such as the retina that lines the back of every human eyeball. When a photon meets such a solid object, it usually deposits its energy in the object, transferring whatever energy it had to that object and disappearing as a result. Some objects are transparent to certain types of photons, allowing them to pass through with little or no effect upon them.

Consider, then, what happens to allow us to see the world. Our eyes have evolved to detect certain types of photons, which we call visible light. Whenever these photons strike one of our retinas, their energy passes to the specialized structures in the retina, called "rods" and "cones," in which the impact produces chemical changes of the molecules that form them. These changes in their turn stimulate the optic nerves that connect the retina to the brain, creating a message that informs the visual cortex in the brain about the photons that have struck the retina. Although we feel none of it, our sight thus consists of a complex process in which, many times per second, the most recent chemical changes in each retina's cells generate a new message along the optic nerve. The brain, constantly receiving messages from both retinas, processes these signals to combine the information from two eyes and shows us a picture of what lies in front of us. We *feel* that we simply see the world, when in fact a highly complicated system receives a host of photons, records their impacts, turns them into nerve impulses, and writes the record of those impulses in our brains. The information contained in the light rays striking our retinas produces an image of the world, with a "read-out time" equal to about $\frac{1}{10}$ of a second. A movie or a television broadcast, which runs about thirty images past our eyes each second, can therefore fool our brains into believing that we see quasi-reality streaming by us, much as the real thing does. Had we a fly's eye, which processes several hundred images per second, we would see movies and television programs as a series of still pictures, with each of them only slightly different from the preceding one.

Although they are not quite so sensitive as those of an eagle or a tiger, human eyes can discriminate between two sources of light spaced only $\frac{1}{60}$ of a degree apart, an angle equal to $\frac{1}{30}$ of the moon's apparent diameter. Of the two types of light-detecting cells in the retina, the cones have the ability to discriminate among colors, while the rods perceive only shapes. Evolution has produced both rods and cones for their specialized purposes: since the rods have an "easier" task, they can detect small amounts of light better than the cones. Under low lighting conditions, we therefore lose our ability to see

Interpreting the Images That Our Retinas Record

The process by which the chemical changes in our retinas create an image in our minds is far more complex than the simple transmission of a picture, like that on photographic film, from the retina to the brain. Experiments have shown that volunteers wearing special eyeglasses that invert beams of light, turning up into down and vice versa, will become highly and understandably disorganized for a time. Within a few days, however, these volunteers' brains will have learned a new way to process the information reaching their retinas, so that the world once again appears in a normal, right-side-up orientation! This could hardly occur if our retinas created an image to be sent as a whole into the visual cortex, for we would then expect that these volunteers would see the world upside down so long as they wore the eyeglasses that inverted the images on their retinas.

colors, and all cats appear black, or at least colorless, in near darkness.

The Great Fall-Off

We all know from experience that if we stand farther from a source of light, it will appear fainter. This occurs because the light rays, in order to reach us from a greater distance, must fill a greater region of space. The laws of geometry, which govern the relationship between volume and distance, require that the apparent brightness of any source of light must decrease in proportion to the *square* of its distance from an observer. If we move the light-emitting object to twice its original distance, the brightness we perceive will fall by a factor of four; if we increase the distance by a factor of three, the object will appear only one-ninth as bright. In physics classes, students are encouraged to make actual measurements that verify this rule, using an instrument that measures the brightness of different sources of light. Lacking any such instrument, but using the measurements recorded by our eyes and brains, we can nevertheless easily see, for example, that automobile headlights seen at a distance of one thousand yards shine only one-quarter as brightly as those seen from five hundred yards away. In a rough-and-ready way, most of us use the relationship between distance and brightness to gauge the distances of other automobiles when we drive on the open highway at night.

JUDGING THE DISTANCES TO STARS

Astronomers have long known that if we observe two stars that produce the same amount of light per second, then the fainter star must be farther from us. If they measure these stars' brightnesses and discover that the fainter one shines with $\frac{1}{25}$ of the apparent brightness of the brighter star, it must be five times farther from us: a distance five times greater produces a diminution in brightness by the square of five, or twenty-five times. By employing relatively arcane methods to establish which stars actually do produce the same amount of light each second, astronomers have used this rule repeatedly to derive the distances to a faraway star once they have measured the distance to a relatively nearby one. If, for example, we find a star that produces the same energy output each second as Sirius, but has a brightness only $\frac{1}{100}$ of Sirius's, we can easily and correctly conclude that this star must have ten times Sirius's distance of 8.8 light years. As we mentioned on page 68, one light year, the distance that light travels through space during a single year, equals approximately 6 trillion miles.

In this vast and glorious cosmos, only some objects emit light, but all of them can reflect, block, or bend the rays of light that happen to strike them. We there-fore see objects either because they emit their own light or because they reflect light from the objects that do produce light.

OBSERVING THE WORLD IN REFLECTED LIGHT

Without regarding our activities as an experiment, we constantly note the difference between the light produced naturally by the sun or artificially by countless indoor light bulbs on the one hand and the light that other objects reflect on the other. We do notice that if we remove all sources that produce light, then we see no reflected light, and that if an object blocks a light source, then a dark region, called the object's shadow, appears on the side opposite the light source. These experiments help to verify the theory that our vision requires a source of light for illumination—a theory that might appear self-evident, but actually underwent a long struggle with a competing theory, that vision arises when *our eyes* generate beams that bounce off the objects we see! Even today, if you query your friends and relatives, you will find some confusion on this point. Superman's x-ray vision involves a similar confusion, for his creators have assumed not only that Superman's eyes could *detect* x rays, but also that his eyes somehow *produce* x rays on their own!

When light strikes an object, some of it will be reflected, while the rest is "absorbed," swallowed out of existence as the photons deposit their energy in the object's surface. Highly polished mirrors reflect more than 99 percent of the light that strikes them, while an asphalt highway reflects only 6 or 7 percent and absorbs the rest. A "perfect absorber," which exists only in theory, would reflect no light at all, and would therefore remain invisible even when exposed to direct illumination. Real objects always reflect some light, which bounces off the object in various directions. It is this reflected light that reveals to us the host of objects that populate our daily lives.

Among the objects in our solar system, only the sun produces its own visible light; we therefore see the moon and the planets solely by their reflected light. Some solar-system objects reflect light far more efficiently than others, adding to their luster in our skies. For example, the moon's surface, made of dark frozen lava and almost equally dark rock, reflects less than 7 percent of the incoming sunlight, blocking or "absorbing" the remain-ing 93 percent without reflecting it at all. In contrast, Venus, perpetually shrouded in a thick atmosphere of carbon dioxide, reflects nearly 70 percent of the incident sunlight, and absorbs almost 30 percent.

Activity One:
Experiment with Light

We can easily recognize the contrast between reflecting light and blocking or absorbing it: reflection simply changes the direction of motion of the rays of light, but absorption consumes light, snuffing it out of existence without a thought for the illumination lost to the cosmos. A third light-altering possibility is refraction, when light rays are bent or "refracted," changing their direction, but typically in small and subtle ways, rather than the large-angle changes involved in most processes of reflection.

Refraction occurs when light passes through a transparent medium such as air or water. Because waves of light travel more slowly in such a medium than they do through empty space, they will change their direction, unless they enter the medium exactly perpendicular direction to its surface. You can observe this phenomenon easily by placing a pencil diagonally in a glass of water and looking at it from various angles. You will see that the part of the pencil that you observe through the water seems to incline at a different angle than the rest of the pencil, which protrudes above the water's surface. Were you a frog hunting prey above and below the water's surface, you would long ago have learned to adjust for this refraction of light.

REFRACTION MAKES THE STARS TWINKLE

This simple experiment finds its analog at every moment of every night as light waves from distant stars penetrate the Earth's atmosphere. There, the effects of refraction produce the most familiar property of the stars, the fact that they twinkle all night long. This twinkling results from the continuous changing refraction of starlight all along the path that it takes through the atmosphere above us. Even on the absolutely clearest night, when you cannot believe that anything lies above you that could hinder the passage of light through the air, your perception deceives you. In fact, the air roils and boils in complex pat-

terns, air currents that move the atmosphere in different directions at different altitudes, creating, in effect, dozens and dozens of air pockets that each bend starlight by a tiny amount. The cumulative effect of these separate refractions makes any star's light appear to arrive from slightly different directions, which change many times per second. This twinkling becomes especially noticeable for the brightest stars, such as Sirius and Arcturus, because your eyes can more easily detect the effects of the continual changes in the paths that the light rays follow as they undergo dozens upon dozens of bendings, during their passage through the atmosphere.

If an object's brightness helps you see it twinkle, why do you see *no* twinkling when you observe the sunlight reflected by the moon and the planets? The answer to this question might seem to have a connection with the fact that you are now observing reflected light rather than light produced by a star. Instead, the difference lies in the *apparent sizes* of the objects that you see. All stars save the sun have such immense distances that they appear to us as single points of light. We therefore observe what amounts to a single beam of light from each of these stars, a beam that undergoes multiple refractions in passing through the air above us. In contrast, all of the planets, distant though they are from Earth and small though they may be in comparison with the stars, have distances from us so much less than the stars' distances that they do have a modest angular size, that is, they appear larger than single points of light. This means that we may conceive of the sunlight reflected by a planet as a set of multiple beams of light. Each of these beams undergoes its own random distortions in passing through the atmosphere. Because these refractions occur in random directions for each beam, adding together all the beams of light—a function that your eyes perform remarkably well in observing a planet—creates a mutual cancellation among the individual refractions, just as the net effect of playing a thousand slot machines in a casino cancels the individuals gains and losses, so that the casino makes a profit every night. The *absence* of twinkling in the light from the moon, Venus, and the other planets reveals to the initiated that these objects must each span an angular distance on the sky sufficient to produce the cancellation of many twinkling beams.

Now that you understand the process of refraction, you are ready to take this knowledge to your observations of the sky. As usual, you will want a night with a clear sky, and if you have a pair of binoculars, these would be handy, although not required. Before using your binoculars, find Venus and compare its light with that from any star. Your naked eye reveals that Venus does have a modest angular size, simply because it does not twinkle. Your binoculars, if you have a good pair, can verify this by showing the modest disk of Venus. In contrast, even the most powerful telescopes show stars only as single points of light. With a simple, careful look at the skies, you have acquired the ability to distinguish planets from stars.

Activity Two:
What Is Color?

If you could carefully examine the different colors contained in the twinkling starlight that reaches your eyes, you would discover an essential fact about the bending of light as it passes through a transparent medium: *different colors bend by different amounts*. Although the differences are small, the twinkling of a star's red light differs from the twinkling of its blue light, so that a star can seem to change color slightly as it twinkles.

Credit for discovering the fact that a medium that transmits light will bend the different colors by different amounts belongs to the great English scientist Isaac Newton. Three and a half centuries ago, Newton performed a now-classic experiment by purchasing a prism, a simple triangular piece of glass that refracts the light passing through it, and using that prism to study the properties of a beam of sunlight in a darkened room. He found that when he passed a beam of "white" sunlight through his prism, the light separated into all the colors of the rainbow, each of which emerged at a slightly different angle, having been bent by a slightly different amount. In his report of 1672 made to the Royal Society of London, Newton stated that the different colors of light can be distinguished by *how much* they bend in passing through a prism. In other words, to paraphrase Newton himself, the least bendable rays exhibit a red color, and red rays are the least bendable, while the opposite holds true at the other end of the spectrum: the most bendable rays are violet in color, and violet rays are the most bendable. This rule applies to all the colors and degrees of bend-

ability between red and violet. Each color will bend by a particular amount by passing through a prism.

Having identified the color of light with the amount of bending that a prism will produce, Newton went on to describe another fundamental fact about color: once separated from its neighbors, each particular color steadfastly maintains that color, resisting all attempts to change it into any other color. Thus, the colors of light each have individual attributes that cannot be transformed or interchanged. This implies that each color effectively represents a slightly different type of light—a fact that has proven to be entirely true, and especially relevant when we look to types of light that our eyes cannot detect (page 108).

A Prism and a Rainbow

To see the different colors of sunlight, I invite you to view light through a prism. If you wish, you may purchase one in a hobby shop, but if you look, you are likely to find a prismatic object in your own home. Do you have a beveled cut drinking glass or vase? A chandelier with hanging crystal, or a diamond ring? Once you have found a prismatic object, place yourself in a sunny window, and move the prism into the beams of sunlight until the light strikes it at the correct angle to produce a mini-rainbow. By projecting this rainbow on the wall, you can see how light always arranges itself in the same spectrum of color, from red to violet. With the knowledge you have gained, take a moment to enjoy the beauty of the visible spectrum and reflect on the delight that we take in colors and their natural arrangement.

As a second excursion into the realm of colored sunlight, I invite you outside after a rain shower, as the sun breaks through the clouds. Here, you are likely to see the demonstration of Newton's laws of optics in that most marvelous phenomenon of light in the atmosphere, the rainbow. Rainbows arise from the combination of reflection, which does not separate the colors of light, and refraction, which most certainly does. When light bounces from a mirror, or from the inside of a raindrop, all colors of light reflect at the same angle. On the other hand, when light passes through a transparent medium, that passage bends the different colors of light by different amounts. Because of this fact, telescopes that focus light by passing it through a lens face the problem that the different colors focus to different points, whereas telescopes that focus light with a mirror, first created by Isaac Newton, bring all colors of light to the same focus point.

Rainbows occur when sunlight reflects from droplets of water, typically soon after, or even during, a light rainfall. You will see a rainbow only when you look in the direction opposite to the sun, because only then will your eyes receive sunlight reflected from the far side of a host of raindrops suspended in the air. These reflected light rays have passed twice through each droplet, first on the way in toward the far side, then, after reflection, on the way out, emerging in the direction that brings them to your eyes. The double passage through the raindrops bends the light rays, and bends each color by a slightly different amount. As a result, you see the full spectrum of color in a rainbow, with red light, which has bent the least, on the outside and violet, which has bent the most, on the inside.

THE COLORS OF THE STARS

Our eyes' inability to detect the colors of faint sources of light makes it difficult for us to see the true colors of the stars. If you turn a pair of binoculars, or a high-powered telescope, toward the clear night

ANOTHER RAINBOW

When you see a particularly fine example of a rainbow, look for a secondary bow of color that arches outside the primary, brighter rainbow. This secondary bow arises from sunlight that has undergone a double set of reflections inside the raindrops; instead of emerging after the first reflection, this light has bounced off the near side of the raindrop while remaining inside the droplet, and then, after passing back to the far side, has reflected off that far side. This set of reflections produces a rainbow in the reverse order of colors, with red on the inside and blue on the outside. The second rainbow is fainter because of the additional reflections that the light rays have undergone. Once in a blue moon, you may even see a triple rainbow, with a third, still fainter bow arching above the first two.

skies, star colors become more evident. You can then see stars shining in brilliant blue, yellow, or orange-red light. Even without any such optical aid, the brightest stars show us their true colors, which in turn reveal fundamental facts about the stars' outer layers, which produce the light that has traveled for tens of trillions of miles to reach our eyes.

Take a look at the bright stars in Orion, along with Sirius to the east of Orion's belt and Aldebaran to the west. Which stars look redder than the others? With reasonably good vision (if all else fails, binoculars will demonstrate this fact clearly), you will note that Betelgeuse, Orion's bright shoulder, wins this contest, with Aldebaran second. In contrast, Orion's bright foot, Rigel, glows bluish-white, as do the three stars in the Hunter's belt. Sirius, on the other hand, seems just plain white, neither bluish nor reddish. The same whitish hue describes the seven stars that form the Big Dipper. Because Sirius is the brightest of all stars, its lack of color cannot arise from a failure of our eyes to perceive the colors of dim stars. Instead, Sirius's hue (or lack thereof), like the colors of the other starry points of light, is explained by differences among the stars.

During the past century, physicists and astronomers came to realize that every star is a giant ball of gas, held together by the gravitational pull that each part of the star exerts on all the other parts. Stars contain such immense amounts of matter that even though their temperatures rise to thousands and millions of degrees, their gravitational forces retain almost all of their hot gases, which would immediately evaporate from less massive objects. These gravitational forces squeeze the star mightily, compressing the hydrogen and helium gas that forms most of its material into conditions of high temperature and density. At the center of a star like our sun, the density rises to ten times the density of gold— yet the matter there remains entirely gaseous! This is so because the temperature rises above 10 million degrees, so hot that the particles in the gas move so rapidly and collide so violently that some of the particles stick or fuse together. The fusion of particles creates new types of matter—and also turns some of the mass of the colliding particles into kinetic energy. Countless collisions among the gas particles slowly diffuse this energy outward. Over about a million years, on the average, the kinetic energy produced by nuclear fusion in a star's core reaches the star's outermost layers, replacing energy that has been radiated from those layers into space.

Every star in the sky therefore represents a giant, natural, nuclear-fusion reactor, capable of shining steadily for millions or billions of years, with particles in the star's core fusing at a steady rate to produce the kinetic energy that heats the entire star as it diffuses outward. On Earth, immense technological efforts to duplicate the sun's nuclear fusion aim at obtaining a cheap source of energy (for hydrogen is abundant on Earth, too) that produces no dangerous waste product. The sun succeeds naturally because of its tremendous gravitational forces, which in turn arise from its enormous mass. In the absence of such forces, we must find other ways to heat and to confine matter raised to temperatures of many million degrees, necessary for nuclear fusion because only then do the particles move fast enough to overcome their mutual repulsion and fuse together. (Hence the attraction of "cold fusion," which would be the greatest thing since sliced bread, if it only worked!)

Some stars perform far more nuclear fusion per second than others, simply because they have more mass. Greater amounts of mass squeeze a star's innards more tightly, producing a higher temperature in the star's core and a consequently greater rate of nuclear fusion. In this case, each point throughout the star becomes hotter than the corresponding point in a star with less mass. This includes the star's outer layers, the regions where the density of gas falls to the point that photons have a good chance of escaping into space. The temperature of the star's outer layers determines the star's color, because it determines the predominant type of photons that exist in these layers. In gas with a temperature of a few thousand degrees Fahrenheit, most of the photons will be red. At temperatures close to 10,000 degrees, the dominant photons will be yellow, and at temperatures of 30,000 degrees or more, violet and blue photons will predominate. Thus, the hottest stars shine with a blue light, while the coolest stars are red. For complex psychological and physiological reasons, we expect the opposite: the hottest objects *should* be red, the coolest blue. Nature, however, has ordered exactly the reverse. Our color confusion may arise from the fact that if we heat an object to the point that it emits light of its own, in a blacksmith's shop for example, that light will be red. If we could only heat the object to still higher temperatures, we would see its light turn successively to orange, to yellow, and finally to blue and violet.

The stars record this pattern faithfully, so that a red star lies at the cool end of the stellar distribution, and a blue-white star ranks among the hottest. Stars that glow with a straight white light, such as Sirius, actually have a peak color in the yellow-green region of the spectrum, but they produce sufficient light of all colors that our eyes and brains record them as just plain white.

Thus, so far as stars are concerned, our eyes and brains provide us with thermometers that can measure the temperatures of objects so distant that their light has taken many years to reach us! By noting the dominant color of an object that produces light on its own, we determine its place in the color arena, the spectrum of color that runs from blue and violet at the hottest end down to red at the coolest end of the panorama of visible light. Whenever you see a star, try to assign it a color, taking the time to let your eyes adapt to the dark and using your peripheral or averted vision as well as a direct line of sight, because (for evolutionary reasons) your peripheral vision often proves slightly superior in sensitivity to your head-on gaze. If the star looks as red as Betelgeuse, its outer layers have a temperature of about 5,000 degrees Fahrenheit (F); if it appears red-orange, like Aldebaran, its light arises in regions with a temperature closer to 6,500 degrees F; a yellow color, reminiscent of our sun's, corresponds to a temperature of about 10,000 degrees F; and a white color like that of Sirius indicates a temperature of 18,000–20,000 degrees Fahrenheit. The hottest, blue-white stars, those that shine like Rigel or the three stars in Orion's belt, have temperatures well above 30,000 degrees, and in some cases touch 50,000 degrees. These superhot stars actually produce most of their energy not in the form of visible light but instead in radiation invisible to human eyes, called ultraviolet. This fact leads us to realize that in order to complete our understanding of the nature of light, we must look beyond the visible and enter other realms of the full spectrum of radiation.

Activity Three:
Beyond Visible Light

Once you have seen the different colors of starlight, and have come to understand the fundamental differences among these colors, you may well ask, Is this all? Can there be colors more bendable than violet, or less bendable than red light? As you probably know, the answer, elucidated throughout the nineteenth and twentieth centuries, has turned out to be a resounding Yes! Light itself, which we do better to call visible light, has turned out to form only a tiny fraction, technically an infinitesimal one, of the full spectrum of what scientists call "electromagnetic radiation."

All electromagnetic radiation resembles light in consisting of photons, particles with a wavelike

nature. Only visible light, however, consists of photons with the set of wavelengths and frequencies that lie within the particular domains to which our eyes respond. This biological definition of light excludes all the other types of electromagnetic radiation, which consist of photons different from those in visible light. How different? They are not different in their most fundamental properties, which exhibit both wave and particle characteristics. If we think of each photon as a particle that vibrates as it moves, we can express the differences among photons as differences in the photons' frequencies, the number of times the photons vibrate each second, and in the photons' wavelengths, the distances that they travel while they vibrate once. Since all photons travel at the same speed, those with higher frequencies (more vibrations per second) must have shorter wavelengths (less distance traveled during each vibration). The photons that we cannot see either have longer wavelengths and smaller frequencies than visible light, as is true for radio, microwaves, and infrared radiation, or else have shorter wavelengths and higher frequencies than visible light, which is characteristic of ultraviolet radiation, x rays, and gamma rays. These names specify different regions within the entire spectrum of electromagnetic radiation, which provides a continuum in which each type of radiation bends into the neighboring types at their boundaries, which are human-defined and are not an essential feature of nature.

OBSERVING ELECTROMAGNETIC RADIATION OTHER THAN VISIBLE LIGHT

Because our eyes cannot detect the other six types of electromagnetic radiation, these types remained almost entirely unknown until the technological advances of the last century and a half. Today, however, we know them all, and have learned how to use them all to our advantage, or, at the very least, to protect ourselves against the harmful types. Let us take a brief tour through the rest of the full spectrum of electromagnetic radiation, noting the good and bad aspects of each.

RADIO WAVES

Radio waves, with the longest wavelengths and smallest frequencies of all types, have proven the most useful (except, of course, for visible light itself) to humanity. Like waves of light, radio waves consist of streams of photons, each of which travels at the speed of light through empty space, and almost as rapidly through the Earth's atmosphere. As a result, these radio-wave photons can be used to carry messages at high speed, not only around the Earth but also between the Earth and distant spacecraft embarked on missions of exploration. Because each photon carries an amount of kinetic energy directly proportional to its frequency, and because energy often corresponds to monetary outlay, at least roughly, radio waves prove the least expensive of all, since they possess the lowest frequencies. The success of radio and television (which consists of pictures and sounds encoded by radio waves) testifies to the economy and ease of manipulation that now characterize society's treatment of the longest-wavelength part of the spectrum of electromagnetic radiation. A further benefit appears in radar (coined as an acronym for RAdio Detection And Ranging), streams of radio waves sent outward in all directions from a transmitter. Aircraft and other flying objects reflect some of these radio waves, and some of the reflected waves return to the point of their creation, where specialized systems detect and analyze them. This reveals both the position and the distance (because the time delay of the radar echo depends on how far the waves travel) to the objects reflecting the waves.

To "observe" radio waves, indulge in that most ordinary activity: turn on your radio or television! Radio waves produced by dozens of different broadcasting stations, each distinguished by slightly different frequencies of vibration, continuously pass through your environment, carrying coded messages of speech, music, and visual images. You cannot feel or detect these waves, but your equipment can—so modern society talks to itself with radio waves.

MICROWAVES

Microwaves, sometimes called submillimeter radiation, are essentially a subdivision of radio waves that includes the radio photons with the shortest wavelengths and highest frequencies. Like radio waves, microwaves participate in our daily routines: most of us employ them to cook food quickly. Whenever you turn on your microwave, your "detector" (the food) records the impact of microwave photons. The process works because the microwaves used for cooking have wavelengths close to the sizes of the molecules in food that contain water. These waves interact most strongly with those molecules, for it is a truism in the physics of waves and particles that a wave will have its largest effects on objects whose size roughly equals the wavelength. This explains, for example, why a ship will find itself most strongly buffeted by waves about as long as the ship itself. By generating microwaves with the appropriately sized wavelengths, we can "zap" the molecules in food so well that a few minutes produces a hot meal.

INFRARED RADIATION

Infrared radiation has frequencies and wavelengths between those of microwaves and visible light. Its name, which means "beyond the red," testifies to the fact that as you pass beyond the longest wavelengths that our eyes can detect, you enter the infrared domain. Where our eyes may fail us, our bodies do not: we sense infrared radiation as heat. Anyone who leans toward a hot stove knows that our skin can sense infrared radiation, not an extremely useful ability because our skin has a rather low sensitivity. The family of snakes called "pit vipers" rely on infrared detectors to locate their prey, even in total darkness, by the heat (that is, the infrared radiation) produced by those animals. No chance on Earth exists for the prey to "hide" by ceasing to produce infrared; the laws of physics state that every object at temperatures significantly above absolute zero will emit detectable amounts of this type of radiation.

If you would like to "see" infrared radiation more directly, a simple experiment suggested by my friend Ken Brecher awaits you. Take hold of the remote control for your television, VCR, or stereo system, and find the plastic dimple that you point toward the instrument in question to change settings. Look at this dimple as you push one of the buttons (a harmless operation): Do you see anything? No? Then we can agree that the remote control does not produce visible light in any significant quantity. Now take one of the inexpensive video cameras (or, if you prefer, take an expensive one) that are becoming ever more common, often mounted on a computer to record the local scene. The detectors in these cameras respond to infrared radiation as well as visible light. Point the plastic dimple toward the camera, and you will see a flash of infrared radiation recorded by the camera every time that you push the remote's buttons.

ULTRAVIOLET, X RAYS, AND GAMMA RAYS

On the other side of the visible-light domain appear the three types of electromagnetic radiation that have higher frequencies and shorter wavelengths than light does, called ultraviolet, x rays, and gamma rays. These are the dangerous types, because their photons carry significantly larger amounts of energy than do radio waves, microwaves, or infrared. (This explains why most scientific studies have failed to show any danger from these low-frequency, low-energy types of radiation, but the verdict remains a bit open, and we would all do well not to nestle too close to our radio-emitting equipment.) Ultraviolet radiation from the sun, for example, causes skin cancer and other harmful effects, and would long ago have killed us all, since the sun emits copious quantities of ultraviolet, if our atmosphere did not block almost all of it from reaching the Earth's surface. Your body will detect more ultraviolet (but mostly without your feeling its effects consciously) if you go to high altitudes, since the thinner air there allows more ultraviolet radiation to penetrate. Even more obvious, now that you know the ultraviolet story, is the fact that we do well not to tamper with the ozone in our atmosphere, which produces most of the blockage of the most harmful kind of ultraviolet, the type whose wavelengths are closest to those of visible light. Ozone consists of oxygen atoms bound into triplets (hence it carries the chemical symbol O_3), an arrangement that provides excellent shielding against the long-wavelength type of ultraviolet radiation. Every reduction in the amount of atmospheric ozone, typically the result of our release of chemicals that combine with ozone molecules and diminish their abundance, raises the risk of skin cancer for the inhabitants of our fragile planet.

X radiation (x rays for short) has a great name, a tribute to the mystery surrounding its initial discovery just over a century ago, when scientists accidentally used a photographic plate to record the x rays emitted by radioactive minerals. We now know that x rays consist of electromagnetic radiation with extremely short wavelengths and high frequencies and energies. These properties allow x rays to penetrate our flesh, though typically not our bones, so that medical personnel can take photographs of our skeletal structures by arranging to produce x rays and to direct them through the tissue to be studied, and then onto a photographic film, or a phosphorescent screen, that records the impacts of the x rays that pass through. Because overdoses of x rays cause an array of harmful results, most of us do well to keep our experiments with medical x rays to a minimum. Our atmosphere, that unsung hero of life on Earth, blocks all the x rays that strike it from outer space, so even great astronomical outbursts, rich in x rays and in the even more harmful gamma rays, cannot affect us by their impacts.

Finally, at the highest-energy end of the electromagnetic spectrum, we meet gamma rays, the most dangerous electromagnetic radiation of all, likewise blocked by our atmosphere. Gamma rays occupy the short end of the wavelength scale and the top of the frequency domain. In nature, some gamma rays arise from the decay of radioactive nuclei such as uranium-235, a fact that argues strongly in favor staying as far as possible from minerals that carry significant amounts of radioactive material. This is one experiment you *don't* want to perform. Our nuclear arsenal contains thousands of weapons that use radioactive nuclei either to produce or to detonate an explosion; although these weapons kill mainly by the enormous outbursts of energy they produce, a lingering effect, equally fatal and highly unpleasant, arises from the gamma rays that appear immediately after the explosion.

Thus seven types of electromagnetic radiation—gamma rays, x rays, ultraviolet, visible light, infrared, microwaves, and radio—fill out the full spectrum, as scientists would say. The recent history of astronomy has seen the glorious opening of this spectrum, including the highest-energy portions and much of the microwave domain, which hitherto remained entirely inaccessible because our atmosphere blocks them all from reaching instruments on the Earth's surface. By sending spacecraft beyond the atmosphere, we have begun to wrest the cosmic secrets embodied in this radiation, both the highest-energy varieties, which speak to us of unimaginable cosmic violence, and the low-energy, microwave sort, which carry the "whisper of creation," the waves created when the universe had less than one one-thousandth of its present age. Here we part company with what we ourselves can see, relying on our alternate, virtual eyes to sweep the spectrum for all the news that the cosmos brings.

MEDITATION

The simple fact that we cannot see gamma rays, x rays, ultraviolet, infrared, microwaves, or radio waves should not compel us to the conclusion that our eyes can inform us about the universe only through what we can see, namely the sources of visible light that shine in the skies above us. One great fact about the cosmos emerges not from light but from darkness. Why, in fact, do we have darkness at night? This question, apparently so simple to answer, conceals a tremendous truth about the cosmos: we have darkness because the universe has not yet grown old.

Darkness, by definition, means the absence of light, a situation quite familiar to us even in the modern era of artificial illumination. Once the sun goes down, we receive relatively little light from the moon, planets, and stars. Unless we flip a switch that allows electricity to course through the wiry veins of our homes and offices, we find ourselves in the dark. How can this simple fact prove anything remarkable? Why should the fact that the sky is dark at night amaze, astonish, or even perturb anyone?

Think a bit farther, and the perturbation will grow. If asked *why* the sky is dark at night, you will surely answer, because the stars are all so far away that none of them shines with anything but a faint brightness in the night skies. Even the large multitudes of stars in the Milky Way galaxy cannot overcome the basic effect of the enormous distances to the stars, a diminution in brightness by a factor of four every time that the distance doubles. But if the universe extends indefinitely, this fact will be exactly balanced by the fact that every time we looked twice as far, we would expect to encounter four times as many stars. To use an analogy proposed by the astronomer Ted Harrison, imagine yourself amid a forest of trees, attempting to see past the forest to the larger world beyond. If the forest has a sufficiently large size, however, *every line of sight that you choose will end at a tree*. Some of these trees will be closer to you and some farther from you, but no matter what their distances, your gaze will encounter nothing but tree trunks.

Now replace the trees with individual stars, and for your view only in directions through the forest, substitute a gaze that encompasses every possible direction. Once again, if the stars go on forever, no line of sight can escape running into a star's surface. Some lines of sight may extend for millions, some for billions, some even for trillions of light years, but eventually you will find a star's surface in every conceivable direction in which you can look. As a result, the entire night sky should glow with a brightness equal to that of a star's surface!

Most assuredly, this does not occur. Why not? The first astronomers to examine this seeming paradox, the Frenchman Jean-Philippe Loys de Chéseaux and the German Wilhelm Olbers, proposed that starlight must be absorbed by invisible dark material in space. This absorption would prevent light from all but the relatively close stars from reaching the Earth, thus preserving the darkness of our night skies. Impressively, de Chéseaux and Olbers thereby deduced, on spurious grounds, the existence of the dark dust that actually does absorb starlight (see page 175). Their reasoning proves faulty in the long run: the absorption of starlight by definition implies the deposition of energy into the dust grains that do the absorbing. This will heat the dust grains until they begin to glow. Eventually, the dust grains will produce as much light each second as they absorb, so that we find ourselves returning to the image of a night sky that glows as intensely as a star's surface.

What, then, can satisfactorily explain the dark night sky? One answer might be that stars do not extend indefinitely into space. Whether they do or not—whether the universe is infinite or finite in its volume and stellar content—remains a mystery, a fit subject for other books and further investigation. However, whether or not the cosmos is infinite in size, it apparently has such an enormous size that this explanation for the darkness at night should not be considered the solution to the problem of nighttime darkness. A different finiteness, however, does the trick: the universe has only a finite *age*. This age, the time since the big bang that began the expansion of the universe, now equals 14 billion years, give or take a billion, according to astronomers' best estimates. Large though this age may seem, it implies that *we can receive light from only those stars and other objects that lie within 14 billion light years of the Milky Way galaxy*. This suffices to resolve the paradox. The stars within 14 billion light years, numerous though they may be (roughly a trillion galaxies, with a total of perhaps a hundred billion trillion stars, lie within this distance), nonetheless contribute only a tiny amount to the brightness of the night sky. Only if we received the light from stars millions and billions of times farther from us than 14 billion light years would the sky glow

with anything like a stellar surface. These immensely distant stars may exist, but the universe's finite age prevents them from contributing—so far!—to the glow of the night sky.

Oddly enough, this correct explanation was first clearly expressed by the great American poet Edgar Allan Poe. In 1848, the year before his death, Poe

This image of the United States, compiled from many satellite photographs, shows how our artificial illumination outlines the coastlines and centers of population, making stargazing much more difficult.

published *Eureka: A Prose Poem*, containing his concepts of how the cosmos is arranged. In this work, Poe posed both the paradox and its solution:

> *Were the succession of stars endless, then the background of the sky would present us an uniform luminosity, like that displayed by the Galaxy—since there could be absolutely no point, in all that background, at which would not exist a star. The only mode, therefore, in which, under such a state of affairs, we could comprehend the voids which our telescopes find in innumerable directions, would be by supposing the distance of the invisible background so immense that no ray from it has yet been able to reach us at all.*

Who among us thinks as deeply as Poe did about the blackness of night? Who could imagine the conclusions that lurk in a simple observation of darkness at night? From such minds come great ideas, which we can admire and appreciate by the light of day.

Chapter *Seven*

The Broad Highway of Life

This photograph of Scorpius and Sagittarius also reveals the light from the milky way. The brightest object in the image is the planet Jupiter, which well outshines Antares, the red star in the heart of the Scorpion, visible to Jupiter's lower right.

Picture yourself three thousand years ago, a resident of ancient Babylon in Mesopotamia, of Memphis by the Nile, or of Mohenjo-Daro in the Indus Valley. Civilization has now advanced to the point that intensive, organized agriculture can sustain cities with ten or even twenty thousand inhabitants, the largest the world has ever seen. Life has become far more orderly and secure since the days when your ancestors foraged and hunted, as most of the world's population still does. But you now bask in a far more advanced culture, replete with gods, myths, secular leaders, and a priesthood. How, then, should you spend your evenings?

You might work on your accounts, if you are a merchant, marking tablets with credits and debits, but the dim light available from oil lamps makes such labors far easier during daylight. You might dine with family, friends, or neighbors, talking over affairs large and small. Almost certainly, you will look at the heavens that arch above you, enveloping your society in patterns of dark and light. These starry patterns, rich in portent, easily visible in the absence of streetlights and neon signs, speak to you of cosmic mysteries, secrets known only to the high priesthood that mediates between heaven and earth.

Most of the adults in your town, whether or not directly engaged in agriculture, have learned the cycles of the heavens, which govern the times of planting, growing, and sowing. The patterns of stars have likewise become so familiar to everyone that you can easily name all the major star groups, and quite possibly the minor ones as well. In fact, you have memorized these star groups to the point that you can describe which ones will rise later in the night, and in which order of precedence—a feat that fails to impress your neighbors, since they can do it for themselves. All of you in this city know intimately the particular portion of the sky that draws special attention as the eternal home of all of the seven objects that move through the houses of the fixed stars. These seven alone change their positions with respect to the stars and to one another: the sun, the moon, and the five lesser lights that the ancient Greeks would name *planets*, meaning wanderers. Surely these wandering lights in the heavens, so evident to sight yet so remote from tangible contact, must influence the events that unfold below them. Those who can predict the positions of the sun, moon, and planets with respect to the stars can therefore foretell what will occur in the land. For decades, the high priests of your community have recorded the motions of these wanderers, discovering the recurrent patterns and cycles that allow them to predict future events. Like all who foretell the future, those who succeed have learned to couch their predictions in suitably vague and majestic language, to emphasize their successes, and to downplay their failures.

Do you as an intelligent citizen really believe that the lights that wander through the heavens govern activities on Earth? Of course you do; everyone does, and nothing makes you question the wisdom accumulated through past decades and centuries of study. On a deeper level, what does this belief imply? Basically, that you accept the codes of conduct of the society in which you live, and on which you depend for your continued existence. Thousands of years must pass before you will face a modern dilemma, the need to reconcile the accumulated lore of our ancestors with what the scientific approach reveals about the cosmos. Today we must recognize that the ancient division between heaven and earth no longer makes sense, for we are part of the universe as surely as the sun, moon, planets, and stars. The old divided model of the cosmos suggested similar divisions between the natural and the supernatural, the earthly body and the cosmic soul. As the anthropologist Joseph Campbell liked to point out, we are still struggling to accept the unity of the cosmos, with all its implications for how we see ourselves in universal terms.

Quite understandably, the rise in scientific knowledge has strongly affected how we perceive the planets in their wanderings through the skies, though these meanderings have continued unchanged. Every society that recorded its observations of the sky has been highly impressed by the changing positions of the planets in the sky. Most of these cultures imagined the vault of heaven to be an overarching structure, carrying the stars around the cosmic center on which we live in a daily cycle of rising and setting. For as long as a society could record, these patterns remained unchanged, with each star maintaining the same position with respect to its neighbors. But the seven moving objects, whose number may well have given rise to the seven days of the week, presented a clear exception. Their wanderings among the starry structure of the heavens could be noted with care, then discussed by those who took it upon themselves to conceive an explanation, or at least a set of rules, for the exceptional motions. From Mexico to Mesopotamia, the intellectual apex of many societies has resided in calculating how to predict the places among the stars in which the wandering planets would appear. This knowledge may have been the product of an elite priesthood, but it diffused, perhaps in a simplified form, among an entire population that cared deeply about the moving lights in the sky.

Today, we can easily share the awe that our ancestors felt when they looked for the planets moving through their starry homes. But without somehow suppressing our modern knowledge, we can never fully recapture their feeling that all of this activity centered on our Earth, around which the gods placed lights in the sky to govern the flow of events below. You never gain something but you lose something, as Thoreau said, and we have had to surrender most of our feeling that the cosmos was made for us, and that its visible manifestations therefore quite naturally will guide us along life's journey.

On the other hand, everyone knows that this belief continues to thrive in the form of astrology, the art of predicting the future from the changing positions of the sun, moon, and planets. Astrology first emerged with vigor in ancient Mesopotamia, where priests looked to the heavens to foretell the future. This activity focused exclusively on the ruler, and only by implication on society at large. The Greeks took over much of this Babylonian astrology and passed their knowledge to the Romans, whose emperors often supported court astrologers in high style, so long as their predictions proved satisfactory. Because Roman society had a somewhat more democratic aspect than most of its

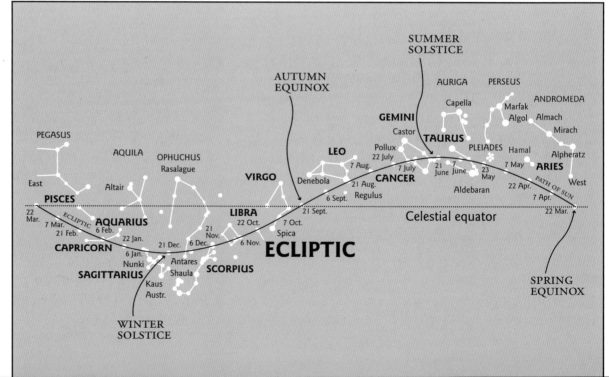

The ecliptic, the sun's path around the sky during the course of the year, can be plotted on a flattened, mercator–like projection of the entire sky. In this projection, the celestial equator runs across the center, and the ecliptic forms a sinuous line above and below the celestial equator. Surrounding the ecliptic are the constellations of the zodiac, which always contain the sun, the moon, and the planets. The dates mark the sun's position as it appears to move along the ecliptic.

predecessors, astrology also spread into the personal realm: for the first time in history, individuals commissioned their own horoscopes, predictions of their futures based on the positions of the sun, moon, and planets at the moment of birth (the word "horoscope" means "a look at the [birth] hour"). Business was brisk in the astrological community, as some of the astrologers' predictions indeed came to pass.

During the past two millennia, astrology has continued to be employed throughout the world, appearing in different formats in cultures from China and Japan to the worlds of Islam and Protestant Europe, but invariably based on the motions of the sun, moon, and planets among the stars. These wandering objects always appear in the twelve constellations that bear the collective name of the "zodiac," derived from the Greek word "zoe," meaning "life," because all but one of them represent animals or demigods.

The twelve zodiacal constellations surround the path that the sun traces through the background of stars during the course of a year. Of course, the Earth, not the sun, does the actual moving, but to us it seems as though we are standing still and that the *sun* is tracing a circle around the sky. Astronomers call this path of the sun the "ecliptic" because eclipses occur only if the *moon* occupies a point precisely on the ecliptic at the time of either full moon or new moon. The division of the stars containing the ecliptic into twelve constellations was made in ancient Babylonia. Because just over 29.5 days elapse from one full moon to the next, the Babylonians, like many other societies, took 30 days, more or less, as their basic subdivision of the year. With approximately 12 months needed to fill up a year, it then must have seemed natural to divide the stars around the zodiac into twelve "houses," so that the sun would spend approximately one month in each of them. On the other hand, ancient Chinese astronomers divided the zodiac not into 12 but into 27 or 28 "moon houses," because the moon takes $27\frac{1}{3}$ days to circle the ecliptic. The difference between this time period and the 29.5-day interval between full moons occurs because the Earth moves around the sun, so the moon must circle a bit farther to regain its full-moon orientation, directly opposite the sun as seen from Earth.

ASTROLOGY AND ITS DISCONTENTS

Any astrological forecast based on the positions of the sun, moon, and planets will concentrate exclusively on the twelve zodiacal constellations, since these include all seven of the wandering objects. (Actually, as described on page 136, the constellation Ophiuchus intrudes into the zodiac, but a purist will dismiss this as an artifact of modern astronomical cartography.) Personal horoscopes take into account not only the positions of the seven wanderers at the time of birth, but also where these objects are today, and where they will be in the future. In early Renaissance times, casting horoscopes for rich people provided significant employment for astronomers, who then stood astride the gap between ancient and modern approaches to the cosmos. Johannes Kepler, for example, who discovered that the planets move in elliptical orbits, also cast many a horoscope. As modern society advanced, however, progressively less was heard about astrology. Neither George Washington nor Abraham Lincoln paid any attention to their horoscopes, which became the province of antiquarians and devotees of the magical arts. The rebirth of astrology in modern times was sparked by the birth of Princess Margaret of England on August 21, 1930. Seeking a means of popularizing the relatively modest nativity of a younger daughter born to the younger son of the reigning British monarch, the *London Sunday Express* blazoned Margaret's horoscope on its front page. This struck such a deep and responsive chord among the public that the newspaper immediately commissioned a series of articles on astrology. Within a remarkably short time, the surge in public interest led to wider employment for astrologers, as well as to the daily astrological columns in thousands of newspapers, whose format was in fact invented by the astrologer who cast Princess Margaret's horoscope for the *Sunday Express*.

The fact that everyone knows the basis of these horoscopes—the "sun sign" or "birth sign" that specifies the constellation in which the sun was located on the day of your birth—testifies to the enduring appeal of astrological prognostication. Your birth sign corresponds to just one of the zodiacal constellations, among which you can also locate the moon and the planets at the time of your birth; these twelve star groups also house the same objects at any other time. The motions of the sun, moon, and planets through the constellations of the zodiac has led to the creation of a marvelous, intricate body of lore, but an astrologer's income, as always, depends on his or her ability to persuade those who pay for the predictions of their validity. Many astrologers have mastered this art, with the result that a telephone conversation with a successful pay-by-the-minute astrologer costs about as much per hour as a face-to-face interchange with a successful lawyer. All scientific testing, typically involving double-blind sets of predictions and assessments, has rejected the hypothesis that horoscopes can successfully predict the future, but the desire to believe that the sun, moon, planets, and stars govern our destiny so far outweighs our desire to assess the matter rationally that many of us look every day at what our newspaper horoscopes have to tell us, and some of us spend real money for personalized, individual horoscopes that go beyond our birth signs.

The depth of our desires in this matter has easily survived the passage of time, though time has so perturbed the astrology created in ancient Babylonia that even if it had been valid then, it would not be valid now. As time goes by, the orientation of the Earth's rotation axis slowly changes, because the Earth has a slow wobble like a spinning top's, caused by the gravitational forces from the moon and the sun. This effect, called "precession," causes the Earth's axis to point toward different parts of the sky in succession (see page 66). Twelve thousand years ago, the bright star Vega stood almost directly above the Earth's North Pole, and furnished an even better north star than Polaris does today. Fourteen thousand years from now, a full, 26,000-year cycle of precession will

end, and Vega will once again be the Earth's north star. The cyclical variation in the orientation of the Earth's axis does not alter the sun's ecliptic path around the sky, but it does change the times of the year when the sun reaches different points along this path, and therefore occupies the different constellations or "houses" along the zodiac. Precession also changes the location of the celestial equator on the sky, the imaginary line that circles the sky halfway between the north and south celestial poles, and therefore causes different parts of the zodiac to lie farthest to the north and to the south of the celestial equator.

In the days of ancient Babylonia, the sun entered the zodiacal constellation Aries on the first day of spring and remained in Aries for the following month. As a result, most horoscopes still say that if your birth date falls between March 20 and April 21, Aries is your birth or sun sign. In fact, the sun now enters Aries early in May. Similarly, *every* birth sign of conventional astrology no longer corresponds to the dates assigned (correctly) to that sign some three thousand years ago. In those bygone days, the sun, as it steadily followed its ecliptic path among the stars, reached its maximum distance to the north of the celestial equator when it stood in the constellation Cancer, and its maximum distance to the south when it was in Capricorn. This gave the names of the "Tropic of Cancer" and the "Tropic of Capricorn" to the latitudes on Earth farthest from the equator where the sun can still appear directly overhead, as it does on June 21 along the Tropic of Cancer and on December 22 along the Tropic of Capricorn. If these names kept pace with reality, we would now refer to the "Tropic of Taurus/Gemini" and the "Tropic of Sagittarius/Scorpius," because the sun's maximal excursions from the celestial equator now occur when it lies at the intersections of those zodiacal constellations.

We can easily live with the old names, and it turns out that most people who believe in astrology, whether minimally or maximally, do so without worrying that their birth signs no longer correspond to the actual locations of the sun along the ecliptic. Many of those who glance at the astrology columns do so with a mixture of belief and skepticism, accepting the positive and rejecting the negative predictions, or accepting those that turn out to be true while rejecting those that do not. Others take the matter far more seriously, and a small minority of astrological devotees have accepted the fact of precession, so that their birth signs no longer correspond to those of conventional astrology. Instead, they agree with the sun and the stars. This has not improved the predictive power of "New Age astrology," as it is called, but it has made that branch of astrology more modern.

In addition to enclosing the sun's path around the sky, the twelve zodiacal constellations also provide the homes of the moon and the planets. We now know the reason why: the planes that contain the orbits of the planets around the sun, and of the moon around the Earth, almost coincide with the plane of the Earth's orbit around the sun, so these planes resemble the nearly parallel pages of a slightly opened book. Whenever you look outward in any direction around the plane of the Earth's orbit, which amounts to looking on the sky in directions along the sun's ecliptic path, your line of sight almost coincides with the planes of the orbits of the other wanderers, the moon and planets. Astronomy and astrology share common origins. Both derive from observing the sky, but astrology (the "logos" or fundamental truth about the stars) seeks to discover what the motions of celestial objects tell us about life on Earth, while astronomy (the "nomos" or naming of the stars) aims at a more cosmic task, that of uncovering the facts about the objects themselves. Both approaches retain a common basis: if you look for the sun, moon, or stars, you will find them in one of the twelve constellations of the zodiac.

Activity One:
Finding the Zodiac in Winter and Spring

Because the zodiac extends all the way around the sky, we can never see more than half of it at one time. Furthermore, because the sun always occupies a position within the zodiac, we usually cannot see either the zodiacal constellation that contains the sun or (except with great exertion) much of the ones that lie immediately on either side. If you want to learn the zodiac, you will do best to divide the task into two halves that depend on the season of the year—an activity that links us to those who first invented the twelve houses, and allows us to enjoy half of the zodiac no matter when we look at the sky.

In the modern world, two serious difficulties confront those who seek the twelve constellations of the zodiac in the night sky. First, city lights have dimmed our view of the heavens, increasing the effort that you must expend to locate groups of not-so-bright stars, an accurate description of more than half of the zodiacal constellations. Second, you must accept the fact that only two, or three at most, of these twelve constellations look anything like the forms that they are held to represent. Though the creatures represented by the zodiacal constellations include a pair of fish, a water-bearer, a goat, a crab, an archer, and a pair of scales, the stars that comprise them show no real resemblance to any of these figures. For many people, locating one of these star groups leads only to a disappointed failure to connect, because such a large gap exists between what ought to be and what is in the sky. Do not let yourself be discouraged because you can't see a fish or a crab! No one can do so—unless he or she employs the power of imagination, the ability to identify our terrestrial life with the stars above.

Our ancestors, who possessed this ability in great abundance, would find absurd anyone's disappointment that Cancer looks nothing like a crab. The gods who ruled heaven and Earth appeared in their starry domain in the ways that they chose; we humans had nothing to do with the matter but to admire and worship them, and to do our best at perceiving their commands. The tales of the gods sank such deep roots into human consciousness that no one objected to the lack of a visual correspondence between the figures of myth and the figures in the sky. Probably just the reverse occurred: the more

difficult the task of identifying the constellation associated with a particular godlike figure, the more worthy the result, and the more credit for the priest who
knew how to make this identification. With a host of
stars to choose among (for without city lights, more
than a thousand individual stars can be seen with a
good pair of eyes), the problem of recognizing the
star patterns of the gods suffered from an embar-
rassment of riches, not the dearth of bright stars that
most of us now confront.

Today, as you strive to locate the twelve houses of
the sun, moon, and planets, you face a somewhat
daunting task, but one that can be accomplished with
ease once you learn to use the bright constellations as
guides to lead you to the faint ones. Five of the twelve
zodiacal star groups are easy to find: Gemini, Taurus,
Leo, Virgo, and Scorpius. Sagittarius is not so difficult,
but recognizing the remaining half dozen proceeds by
orienting yourself with the brighter six, or with other
constellations close to the zodiac, which will guide
you toward the elusive spondulix.

Finding the zodiac is easiest during the winter and
spring, when Orion stands tall in the sky and offers an
easy means of finding Taurus the Bull and Gemini the
Twins. As we saw in chapter 5, Orion's belt points the
way toward the V that forms the Bull's horns, and the
line from Orion's bright foot through his bright shoulder leads you into the two parallel lines of stars, each
terminating in a particularly bright star, that form the
Twins. When you contemplate the point in the sky
where Gemini runs into Taurus, you will note that
Orion's uppermost stars, which form part of the cloak
that the Hunter flings above his head, almost qualify
as part of the zodiac. This region of the sky where
three fine constellations meet gains additional importance from the fact that here the zodiac intersects the
milky way (see page 130).

With Gemini well identified, you can easily look
to the east of the Twins to find Leo, if you are observing late on a winter night or at any time during the
spring, by finding Regulus, the brightest star in the
Lion. One way to do so is to follow the line from
Orion's belt through Procyon, the bright star in the
Little Dog, which takes you to Regulus once you
extend that line for a bit more than the distance you
covered in passing from the belt to Procyon. The second way to find Regulus, which allows you to certify
your discovery, uses the second set of pointer stars in

the Big Dipper, the ones in the bowl of the Dipper closest to the handle (see page 69).

Regulus lies almost exactly on the ecliptic, the sun's path through the skies that runs through the center of the zodiacal constellations. This first-magnitude star marks the Lion's forepaws, with the sickle-shaped head of the Lion rising from Regulus toward the north celestial pole, and the triangle of the Lion's hindquarters to the east of Regulus, in the direction opposite to Gemini (see page 70). With Leo, you have now found three of the twelve zodiacal constellations, and can proceed to look for the one you skipped over: Cancer the Crab, which lies halfway between Regulus and the two stars that form the heads of the Twins, Castor and Pollux.

Cancer is one of the prime zodiacal losers, so far as bright stars go: none of its stars shines as brightly as any of the *ten* brightest stars in Orion! With good eyes on a dark night, however, you can see five or six of Cancer's stars. Three of them form an equilateral triangle whose base runs from east to west, while the others provide a short line of stars that extends northward from the star at the vertex of this triangle closest to the north celestial pole. If all else fails, stare at the region halfway between

THE BEEHIVE CLUSTER

From a brightness-chauvinist's viewpoint, none of Cancer's stars merits much attention; you can win bets with even the most experienced astronomers by challenging them to produce the actual name of any star in Cancer. Instead, they will cite Cancer's claim to fame, the fine cluster of stars at its center, close to the star at the northern vertex of its starry triangle from which a line of faint stars extends northward. This star cluster, called either Praesepe (the "manger" or "cradle" in Latin) or the Beehive Cluster, lies at the midpoint of an imaginary line between Regulus and the waist of the more southerly of the two Twins, the first star visible in Gemini as you look from Pollux down toward Orion. With normal eyesight, you can see this cluster on any reasonably fine dark night, shining as brightly as the stars in the Crab. A good pair of binoculars will reveal several dozen stars in the Beehive, as Galileo's telescope did four centuries ago, allowing him to be the first to understand the basic nature of this star cluster. Like Regulus, the Beehive Cluster lies almost exactly on the ecliptic, and Chinese astronomers used it as a significant reference in point in recording the motions of the sun, moon, and planets.

Regulus and Castor and Pollux in the Twins, and insist to yourself that you can see stars there.

Thus, in passing from Taurus to Leo, you have visited four of the zodiacal constellations, encountering Gemini and Cancer between the first two. The next toward the east, Virgo, provides no difficulty of recognition. The largest of all the zodiacal constellations, Virgo spreads over nearly 50 degrees of the sky to the east and west of its brightest star, Spica, which lies at the end of the great curve extending from the Big Dipper's handle down through Arcturus and so onward into Virgo (see page 71). If all the constellations had dimensions like Virgo's, only seven or eight of them could fit into the circle of the zodiac. The Virgin's great size implies that the sun spends much more than one month in passing through Virgo, just as it spends less than a month in Cancer or Libra or Aries. If astrology were valid, this might be worth taking into account in casting horoscopes.

Activity Two:
Finding the Zodiac in Summer and Fall

As spring becomes summer, those who seek the zodiac must look farther to the east, past Virgo to the

VIRGO

Virgo, the only female among the twelve constellations of the zodiac, was linked to the goddess of fertility in Egypt and Mesopotamia; her brightest star, Spica, was identified as a spike of wheat, and named after it throughout the Middle East and Europe. Virgo fills nearly all of the area immediately south of Arcturus; most of its stars lie closer to the north celestial pole than Spica does. Sad to say, the Virgin offers no convincing star patterns, and you will do better to enjoy her easy, reclining grace without asking just what orientation she has assumed.

constellations that rise behind it. First comes Libra the Scales, not an easy star group to recognize, but next around the zodiac we find Scorpius the Scorpion, arguably the constellation whose arrangement of stars best justifies its name. To locate Libra, you should therefore first find Scorpius, a much easier and more enjoyable activity.

The half of the zodiac that stretches from Virgo to Pisces lies to the south of the celestial equator. For observers in the northern hemisphere, this poses a modest problem, because the southern constellations do not rise as far above the horizon as the northern ones do. To see Scorpius, you must pick a spot with a good view of the southern horizon, and look to the south near midnight in July, or a couple of hours earlier in August, or soon after sunset in September. Scorpius attracts easy attention for the red supergiant star Antares, which provides its bright red heart, and for its long, fishhook tail, which extends southeastward from Antares, first plunging down toward the horizon, then running parallel to it, and

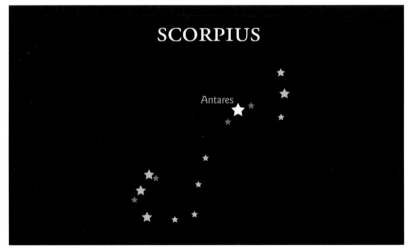

SCORPIUS

Antares

Scorpius has its brightest star, Antares, in the Scorpion's heart. Above Antares lie the three stars in a row that represent the Scorpion's head and claws. Below the heart, the Scorpion's fishhook tail terminates in a close pair of stars.

then turning briefly upward in a northerly direction, ending with a pair of closely-spaced, relatively bright stars that make the identification certain. Once you have found Antares and the Scorpion's tail, look from Antares toward the northwest, in the direction opposite to the tail, and you will soon encounter three bright stars in a line perpendicular to the one you are following. These three stars provide a subdued copy of the three stars in Orion's belt, since they do not shine so brightly and are spaced more widely apart. However, you will have to rely on your memory to compare Orion's belt with the three stars to the northwest of Antares, because Orion and Scorpius, which occupy nearly opposite points on the celestial sphere, can never be seen at the same time (see page 85).

The three stars to the northwest of Antares are often called the Scorpion's claws, or perhaps his two claws and his head, since they lie in roughly the proper position for these roles with respect to Antares at the Scorpion's heart. But the Scorpion's true claws are still farther from Antares. If you extend a line from Antares through the central star in the line of three, and continue outward for a somewhat greater distance than the one you have just traversed, you will come to four modestly bright stars that form a slightly cockeyed diamond. This is the most visible part of Libra, the Scales or the Balance, made of all the stars between Scorpius and Virgo. The two brightest of the four stars, namely the one that lies farthest from Antares and the one at the top of the diamond, have the Arabic names Zubenelgenubi and Zubeneschemali, respectively, meaning "the southern claw" and "the northern claw." If you add these stars to the already sizable constellation of Scorpius, you can imagine an even larger scorpion, with suitably enormous claws rather than the truncated ones furnished by the three stars in a line to the northwest of Antares. This approach, however, would define Libra out of existence.

Scorpius appears at its finest in July and August, though even while crossing the meridian the constellation never rises high in the sky, and its fishhook tail often vanishes in the murk above the southern horizon. When Scorpius is visible, you can use it easily to identify Sagittarius the Archer, just to the east of Scorpius, a relatively compact group of eight or nine stars at the same altitude above the horizon as the lower half of the Scorpion. With an effort, you might persuade yourself that you can actually see a centaur

aiming an arrow toward Scorpius, but if you want to give your imagination a rest, remember that the familiar name for the central part of Sagittarius—the part that you can see without binoculars—is the Teapot. Indeed the stars that you can see do resemble a teapot, with two stars that provide the tip of the spout on one side and the tip of the handle on the other side of the main teapot mass, the side toward Scorpius.

At the boundary between Scorpius and Sagittarius, the ecliptic, the path of the sun through the stars, reaches its southernmost point, exactly opposite its northernmost point at the Taurus-Gemini boundary. At almost precisely this place in the sky, the milky way crosses the ecliptic. Furthermore, when you look toward this meeting point of the ecliptic and the milky way, you are staring almost exactly toward the center of the Milky Way galaxy. (Astronomers use capital letters for the name of our galaxy, lower-case ones for the band of light it produces that shines around the sky.) If you take a pair of binoculars out on a good night, you can see a host of star clusters near the Scorpius-Sagittarius boundary. If it seems as though these clusters come by the dozen, you are correct! If you look sufficiently carefully, you can also spot places on the sky that seem remarkably black, almost devoid of stars. Here you have found dark interstellar clouds, rich in obscuring dust, the potential nurseries of stars waiting to be born.

From the starry richness of Scorpius and Sagittarius, we must confront the relative paucity of stars in the last four zodiacal constellations. These star groups, visible in late summer and fall, can be found with the help of the much brighter constellations that dominate the skies in those seasons. In a way, the relative absence of bright stars makes the task easier, for you need not master the wealth of lights produced by Orion and its neighbors. Instead, the key to the skies of summer and fall lies in the three bright stars of the Summer Triangle. These three can hardly be missed, for they pass close to the overhead point (Vega, the brightest of the three, does pass overhead for observers at latitudes close to 40 degrees north) and dominate all surrounding regions in brightness.

The three stars are Vega, in Lyra the Lyre; Deneb, in Cygnus the Swan; and Altair, in Aquila the Eagle. From June through November you will find them above the horizon, with Vega the brightest, Deneb next, and Altair third. All are first-magnitude stars,

and along with Arcturus, Spica, and Antares are the only first-magnitude stars you are likely to see (with one exception) on summer and fall nights, until once again Aldebaran and Capella, Betelgeuse and Rigel, Pollux, Procyon, and Sirius rise in the evening as

The three bright stars forming the Summer Triangle are Vega (top left), Deneb (far left), and Altair (right center).

autumn draws to a close. The Summer Triangle has a shape somewhat elongated from equilateral, with the line from Vega to Deneb forming its shortest, northern side, so that Altair lies considerably farther to the south than the other two stars. Of the three constellations dominated by these stars, Lyra and Aquila offer little to convince you that you are seeing a Lyre or an Eagle. The Lyre nestles close to Vega, made of seven additional stars (if the night and your eyesight are in good condition) that fill Vega's immediate neighborhood in the direction toward Aquila and Cygnus, and take the shape of a lyre for those who enjoy seeing this as so.

The three stars of the Summer Triangle not only help to identify their constellations but also offer the key benefit of guiding us to the zodiacal constellations of summer. A line from Vega through Altair, extended onward past Altair for the same distance, brings you into the constellation Capricornus the Goat, or Capricorn, as we anglicize his name. Although Capricorn gives Cancer and Aries a good fight as the least visible constellation of the zodiac, it received far more attention than the other two from ancient cultures, who managed to see a goat in a nondescript group of a dozen not-so-bright stars, whose roughly triangular distribution resembles the shape of a boat, a box, or the body of an animal. Even so, Capricorn does a better job of representing its figurative subject than the next zodiacal constellation, Aquarius the Water-Bearer. You can put yourself in Aquarius by following the path from Vega that bisects the line joining Deneb and Altair, and then proceeding in this direction about half again as far as the distance from Vega to the Deneb-Altair line. You will, with luck, find a straggly line of stars that protrudes into the region between Capricorn and Aquila (so that to decide which faint star belongs to Capricorn and which to Aquarius demands expert knowledge) and also extends a long way toward the east, where its faint stars merge with the faint stars in Pisces. If you cannot see a single star in Aquarius, do not count yourself unlucky; its brightest star is only as bright as the ninth-brightest star in Orion.

To find the final two constellations of the zodiac, Pisces and Aries, you will do well to locate first another large, helpful group of stars: Pegasus the Flying Horse. Pegasus lies far from any first-magnitude stars, so you can easily find its four second-magnitude stars, which form a rectangle somewhat misleadingly called the "Great Square of Pegasus", especially recognizable by the fact that the interior of the rectangle contains almost no stars visible without straining. To locate Pegasus, first take a good look at Cygnus, the Swan, made of a long row of three stars for his body, with a star on either side of the central star to provide the swan's wings. The swan's long neck extends from this central star, Sadir, which lies at the center of the Swan's breast, to Albireo in his head. Deneb, in the opposite direction from Albireo, represents the swan's tail. Now imagine a line from Vega that cuts the swan's neck in two, and extend it onward for three times the distance from Vega to the neck. This will bring you to the southwest corner of Pegasus's Great Square. Directly to the south of this corner of Pegasus lies one end of Pisces the Fish, another long, unimpressive group of stars similar to Capricorn's in near-invisibility. Pisces extends all the way below Pegasus and then well to the east, still to the south of Pegasus's Great Square, before it turns northward, with its final stretch directly to the east of Pegasus. If you can perceive this as a fish, or as a pair of fish, you are better at the zodiac game than most. To see two fish, the trick is to imagine their tails tied together at the point where the line of stars turns to the north, so that one fish's head lies due east of Pegasus and the other far away, southwest of Pegasus's Great Square.

Finally we meet Aries the Ram, whose three or four visible stars lie due east of Pegasus's Great Square, past the upturned dim line of the last stars in Pisces. If you have your doubts about whether you have located Aries (and these doubts will be well founded if you are relying on finding any bright stars in the constellation), wait until late in the fall, when you can see Orion and Aldebaran. The line from Betelgeuse, Orion's bright shoulder, through Aldebaran will take you into Aries if you extend it past Aldebaran for a bit more than the distance that you cover in passing from Betelgeuse to Aldebaran. Aries's two brightest stars, Hamal and Sheratan, are fairly close in the sky, and may well be the only stars that you see in the constellation. Thus, if you can find two medium-bright stars at the end of the line from Betelgeuse through Aldebaran, rest content that you have found the Ram, whose first visit from the sun once marked the beginning of spring.

GREAT SQUARE OF PEGASUS

PISCES

AQUARIUS

CAPRICORN

On clear fall nights, observers in the United States can see the "Great Square" of the constellation Pegasus rising high above the southern horizon. To the south of Pegasus are three faint constellations of the Zodiac—Pisces, Aquarius, and Capricorn.

The Second Crossing

In the part of Pisces close to Aries, at an utterly inconspicuous location among faint stars, the ecliptic makes its second crossing of the celestial equator, halfway around the celestial sphere from the point in Virgo where these two great circles also intersect. This crossing in Pisces marks the vernal, or spring, equinox, the location of the sun at the moment that spring begins. In Babylonian times, this point lay on the other side of Aries, where the Ram meets the Bull. With the passage of nearly three millennia, the effects of precession (described on page 123) have altered the position of the celestial equator, so that the sun, moving steadily as always around the ecliptic, now crosses the celestial equator from south to north on March 20, 21, or 22. Historically, the spring equinox marked the start of the year, quite a reasonable approach in societies based on agriculture, though the actual date of March 25 was chosen in much of western Europe. The switch from the Julian to the Gregorian calendar, which occurred in Catholic Europe during the sixteenth century but in England only in 1751, also changed the date of new year, so that you must examine with care any dates in history earlier than this changeover to be sure that you have not confused the years as we define them with those then in common usage.

After Aries comes Taurus, so you have now circled the sky, passing through the twelve zodiacal constellations that made our ancestors sit up and take notice, or, to be more precise, that they made up to take notice of the motions of the wanderers through the heavens. Though Scorpius, Sagittarius, Virgo, Leo, Gemini, and Taurus would draw considerable attention by themselves, Cancer, Libra, Capricorn, Aquarius, Pisces, and Aries would remain utterly obscure among the eighty-eight constellations of the sky, were it not for the fact that they embrace the ecliptic and therefore contain the sun, moon, and planets for half the year.

Activity Three:
Finding the Planets within the Zodiac

The payoff for your efforts in locating the twelve constellations of the zodiac resides in the certainty that if you look for any of the sun's planets, as well as for the sun or the moon, you will find them in one of the zodiacal star groups. The exception to this rule, arising from the constellation boundaries that astronomers have drawn, appears at the boundary between Scorpius and

Sagittarius, near that highly interesting region of the sky where the zodiac, the ecliptic, and the milky way all meet. Here, the constellation Ophiuchus (oh-fee-OO-cuss) the Serpent-Bearer intrudes his nether regions between the Scorpion and the Archer, with the result that by astronomers' reckoning, nearly 20 degrees of the ecliptic resides in Ophiuchus, so the sun spends more than two weeks in this strangely named group of stars—a dynamite bit of information for revisionist astrologers who dare to capitalize on this little-known fact. But perhaps we can do as the ancients did (and does not astrology rest on ancient knowledge rather than on modern attempts to impose a stricter logic on the cosmos?), and insist that Sagittarius and Scorpius must between them embrace that portion of the ecliptic, with Ophiuchus, shorn of his feet, kept safely to the north.

If we do so, the burning question becomes, which planets appear in which constellations, and when? This was the question that made the careers of astronomers for several millennia, as they observed, recorded, predicted, and calculated the planets' positions in the zodiac, first tentatively, then with relative ease and impressive accuracy. They noted the baffling behavior of the planets, especially of Mars, Jupiter, and Saturn, which would move for a time in one direction (eastward)

through the zodiac; then stop, reverse their motion for a time; stop again, and then resume their usual eastward motion. When the Renaissance came to Europe, astronomers with a foot in the modern and ancient ways of understanding the cosmos used these observations to conclude that the planets all move in elliptical orbits around the sun.

For those who simply want to find the planets in the sky, the model that predicts planetary positions becomes irrelevant, so long as the positions that it specifies prove to be accurate. Chapter 3, which describes the motions of Venus, includes a diagram showing where that brightest of planets can be found (though it does so by showing Venus's position with respect to the sun, not by naming the zodiacal constellation in which the planet appears). Mercury, always so close to the sun that you will have some difficulty in finding it, will be left for a more advanced work. That leaves, among the planets visible to unaided eyes, Mars, Jupiter and Saturn. Let us name the constellations where you can find those three.

Saturn takes fully thirty years to orbit the sun, and therefore spends 2.5 years, more or less, in each of the zodiacal constellations. This makes finding Saturn an easy task: until the end of 2002, Saturn will be in Taurus, and from then until July 2005 in Gemini.

Jupiter, orbiting the sun once every twelve years, resides conveniently for just one year, on the average, within each star group along the zodiac. Until August 2002, the sun's largest planet will appear in Gemini; then, until August 2003 in Cancer; from then until September 2004 in Leo, and after that until October 2005 in Virgo. (Leo and Virgo keep Jupiter for a bit longer than one year because of their large sizes.) Thus, both Saturn and Jupiter will be well placed for viewing during the late fall, winter, and early spring.

It is Mars that is hardest to find, Mars the pesky red planet, Mars the signifier of war and destruction, Mars whose motions baffled astronomers for centuries. Today we have tamed Mars in our minds, unraveled its wanderings, touched and tested its soil with our automated emissaries. If you want simply to *see* Mars, the table below shows the constellations, month by month, in which the red planet will appear. These entries refer to the planet's location at the midpoint of each month; at the beginning or end of a month, Mars may be located in one of the neighboring constellations. During the year 2003, from the middle of June through the end of November, Mars, which will then be at its brightest and most easily visible, will spend 5.5 months in Aquarius. During this time, as the Earth overtakes

Mars in its orbit, the planet will slow its motion, stop, reverse itself, accelerate, slow again, stop once more, and then resume its normal eastward motion among the stars. All of this will occur when Mars lies almost directly opposite the sun on the sky, and therefore rises close to sunset and stays up nearly all night. As is its habit, the planet will demonstrate a similar set of motions two years and two months afterward, in late 2005 and early 2006, when it spends 7.5 months in Taurus and Aries. No wonder our ancestors paid homage to the strange movements of the red planet!

A MARTIAN CALENDAR SHOWING THE CONSTELLATIONS IN WHICH MARS APPEARS

*The * sign denotes months in which Mars is too close to the sun on the sky to be easily visible.*

Month	Year	Zodiacal Constellation
November	2001	Capricorn
December	2001	Aquarius
January	2002	Pisces
February	2002	Pisces
March	2002	Aries
April	2002	Taurus

Month	Year	Zodiacal Constellation	Month	Year	Zodiacal Constellation
*May	2002	Taurus	May	2004	Gemini
*June	2002	Gemini	June	2004	Gemini
*July	2002	Cancer	*July	2004	Cancer
*August	2002	Leo	*August	2004	Leo
*September	2002	Leo	*September	2004	Leo
*October	2002	Virgo	*October	2004	Virgo
November	2002	Virgo	*November	2004	Virgo
December	2002	Libra	December	2004	Libra
January	2003	Libra	January	2005	Scorpius
February	2003	Scorpius	February	2005	Sagittarius
March	2003	Sagittarius	March	2005	Sagittarius
April	2003	Capricorn	April	2005	Capricorn
May	2003	Capricorn	May	2005	Aquarius
June	2003	Aquarius	June	2005	Pisces
July	2003	Aquarius	July	2005	Pisces
August	2003	Aquarius	August	2005	Aries
September	2003	Aquarius	September	2005	Taurus
October	2003	Aquarius	October	2005	Aries
November	2003	Aquarius	November	2005	Aries
December	2003	Pisces	December	2005	Aries
January	2004	Pisces	January	2006	Aries
February	2004	Aries	February	2006	Taurus
March	2004	Taurus	March	2006	Taurus
April	2004	Taurus	April	2006	Gemini

MEDITATION

The zodiacal star groups offer a challenge to your imagination far deeper than the task of finding these constellations, even those made of faint stars, in the sky. Can you think your way into the mind-set of your ancestors, who perceived the zodiac not simply as a group of stars, but as a broad highway of demigods along which the guardian lights of Earth moved their mystical ways? Historians always caution the uniniti- ated against projecting our worldview onto those who lived in bygone eras, imagining that they regarded the world much as we do. On the other hand, our ances- tors were certainly human, driven by emotions and desires similar to our own. Can you find the middle ground in imagining a world in which the sun, moon, and planets have been created for the fundamental purpose of cosmic signifiers for humanity? The middle ground, that is, between rejecting this attitude as no more than an incorrect view of the cosmos, and the belief that you can put yourself entirely into the mind- set of your forebears, because you too can perceive a vast cosmic purpose in everything that exists. Our ancestors indulged in no such "modern" religious thought: for them, the Earth was the sole realm beneath the sun, moon, and stars, which had an entirely separate nature.

A poll might well show that in their hearts the majority of all humanity still regards this last conclu- sion as correct. In the United States, Europe, and Japan, however, it has become very much a minority view. Most Christian and Jewish fundamentalists have adapted themselves to the modern discovery that the cosmos consists of stuff much like the Earth, and hardly centers on our small planet. A good argument can be made that no one who has learned this news can ever recover the deep feeling of order and tran- quility that comes from the certain knowledge that the heavens were made for man. This belief, nurtured by all members of society, subjected to no skeptical scrutiny, and unchallenged by any dissent, helped humanity to organize itself and thus, perhaps para- doxically, to advance to the stage in which we now live, with the belief that we rule the sole land that heaven governs gone forever. Of the challenge posed by this disappearance, Joseph Campbell wrote, "All the theological notions based on the distinction between the heavens and the earth collapse with [the realization that they consist of the same sort of matter]. There is a unity in the universe and a unity in our experience. We can no longer look for a spiritual order outside of our own experience."

To most, Campbell's pronouncement seems extreme. Millions still believe in the spiritual order that Campbell claimed no longer to be on the map.

But his words remind us of how much has changed since humanity first identified the stars of the zodiac, and of the difficulty that anyone faces who tries to return in imagination to the days when the sun, moon, and planets ruled the Earth below.

Chapter *Eight*

Heaven in a Grain of Sand

In 1996, NASA scientists announced that this meteorite, discovered in Antarctica in 1984, had reached Earth after being blasted from the surface of Mars.

Seek ye the stuff of heaven? Then touch the Earth. Just over four and a half billion years ago, our planet coagulated itself into existence, collecting its material, as the other planets did, from the pancake-shaped cloud of dust and gas that orbited the still-contracting sun. All matter on Earth, ourselves included, owes its elemental composition to the ten billion years of cosmic evolution that preceded the formation of the solar system. Long before the sun and its planets began to form, hosts of aging and dying stars throughout the Milky Way puffed and spewed into space some of the matter they had processed through their nuclear furnaces. This material enriched the cosmic mulch from which new objects could form, seeding it with the elements heavier than hydrogen or helium. Atoms of the different elements linked together to form molecules; simple molecules combined into more complex varieties; 4.6 billion years later, we contemplate the cosmos as organisms embodying trillions upon trillions of molecules, every one of which contains atoms made inside stars that died billions of years before the Earth was born.

The wide variety of these star-made atoms and molecules has allowed life to originate and to flourish on our planet. During its four billion–year history, life on Earth has evolved through competition as the individual members of each particular species sought to maximize the number of their descendants. In this competition, random variations in the genetic material of living organisms, called "mutations," allow natural selection to discriminate among the mutations that prove harmful, helpful, or neutral as organisms struggle for reproductive success. Like the elements themselves, an important mechanism for producing mutations also arises in the stars. Cosmic-ray particles produced by exploding stars—electrons, protons, and helium nuclei accelerated to nearly the speed of light—continuously bombard the Earth, occasionally provoking the mutations that drive evolution onward. Thus we are living upon the product, as the product, and by the product of the stars. William Wordsworth had it right when he wrote:

> To see a world in a grain of sand,
> And a heaven in a wild flower,
> Hold infinity in the palm of your hand,
> And eternity in an hour.

Wordsworth meant these lines to be a paean to nature, but if you read them as instructions, they encapsulate the history of the cosmic evolution that brought us here.

Activity One: *Touch the Earth*

We spend our days in contact with solid objects such as chairs or beds, rarely asking ourselves what type of matter supports us. Leaving aside the host of different types of material processed into existence by our technological capabilities, let us go to the local heart of the matter. Take yourself outside for a short walk, check for human-made dangers, and pick up a handful of soil. We are almost all familiar with this stuff that Earth is made of; if you have a propensity toward working in your garden, you're used to having it under your fingernails. As children, we were more inclined to interact with this stuff than you may be now—rolling in it, making mud pies, getting "dirt"-y. Today, grab some dirt and reflect that you are holding a handful of the outermost layer of our home planet. What is it made of?

What you hold in your hand is a mixture of different types of rock, some of it ground exceedingly fine by the action of wind and weather. Put differently, you hold the result of 14 billion years of cosmic evolution, of which the first two-thirds occurred before the Earth formed, together with the sun and its other planets, 4.6 billion years ago. When the Earth came into existence, it acquired a mixture of elements, most of which had already condensed into a solid state before joining our planet-in-formation. If we lived on the moon or Mars (but it is no accident that we do not!), we could find rocks nearly as old as 4.6 billion years by taking a stroll and gathering samples at random. There, with neither erosion nor the motions of continental plates to alter them, individual rocks have remained unchanged for billions of years. Indeed, most of the rock samples brought to Earth by the astronauts who visited the moon between 1969 and 1972 have ages greater than those of *any* rock found on Earth.

What happened to Earth's ancient rocks? A look around you provides a portion of the answer, though not the most significant part. We live not on a sterile planet but on one rich in atmospheric activity, with cycles of rainfall, runoff, and evaporation by which water continually carves the land into new shapes. These cycles of rainfall, together with cycles of freezing and melting in the middle latitudes, slowly erode all rocks, carving and cracking them into new forms.

AS THE SEA FLOOR SPREADS, THE CRUSTAL PLATES SLIP, SLIDE, AND COLLIDE

The most significant geological processes lie beyond our time horizon, operating so slowly that a human lifetime allows us only a snapshot. Beneath all of Earth's large bodies of water, rocks are slowly forming from the fine rain of sediments that settles downward onto the sea floor. Left to themselves, these sedimentary rocks would line the ocean bottoms, forever hidden from our view and unimportant in our daily lives. Geological activity on Earth, however, tells a different story. On time scales measured in millions of years, our planet's surface bumps and grinds its way to new configurations, raising dry land where once oceans ruled and sinking continents into the oceans again.

The driving force behind this activity occurs near the centers of the ocean floors, where hot volcanic material wells upward through the thinnest parts of the Earth's crust. This hot magma spreads the sea floors, forcing the ocean bottoms apart. For ten thousand miles, the mid-Atlantic ridge runs beneath the North and South Atlantic Oceans, made of upwelling material that gradually pushes the Americas still farther from Europe and Africa. Even today, tens of millions of years after they separated, we can see a reasonable match between the coastlines on either side of the Atlantic—a match that grows better if we map not the sea-level coastlines but the edges of the continental shelves, where the shallow waters offshore drop steeply into the ocean depths. If you want to see sea-floor spreading close-up, take a trip to Iceland, where the mid-Atlantic ridge breaks the surface. There, where a host of volcanoes have changed the landscape, you will find new islands being born out of lava rising from below.

Because the sea floor spreads, the plates that form the Earth's crust move slowly against and over one another. Where they do so, earthquakes and volcanoes appear far more often than elsewhere, though

YOUNG ISLANDS

You might conclude from their volcanic activity that the Hawaiian Islands in the mid–Pacific Ocean likewise lie along a sea-floor-spreading ridge, but in fact this conclusion is invalid. Sea-floor spreading in the Pacific Ocean occurs in complex patterns that often approach the continents. The Hawaiian Islands lie atop a "hot spot," a weak point in the continental plate through which lava emerges as the plate slowly moves above it. As the plate has slipped slowly toward the west, the hot spot has built each of the Hawaiian Islands in turn, from Kauai and Niihau, the oldest and westernmost, to the Big Island of Hawaii, the youngest and by far the most volcanically active in the chain. East of Hawaii, miles beneath the surface, the new island of Loihi is forming, ready to appear within the next million years or so, when the seamount breaks the calm Pacific surface with explosions far greater than any that now occur on the Big Island. The world's greatest observatory rests atop Mauna Kea, the largest of the volcanoes that made Hawaii, now dormant—may it continue to be so!

no part of Earth can be judged perfectly safe from either type of event. In California, the San Andreas fault rules the network of fractures in the plate that supports most of the state. West of the San Andreas, however, lies the Pacific Plate, upon which the south-westernmost parts of California repose. As the Pacific Plate slowly grinds its way northward, it causes continual readjustments near the plate boundary, producing earthquakes large and small. All around the shores of the Pacific Ocean, a "ring of fire" marks the plate boundaries with volcanic eruptions and earthquakes, so that Japan, Alaska, and Chile, among other regions, experience these phenomena noticeably more often than the interiors of the continents do.

As the plates move, they bury rocks far below the Earth's surface, squeezing them with huge amounts of force that affect the molecular structures within the rocks. Geologists classify all rocks into three types: igneous or fire-formed rocks, which emerge from volcanic eruptions; sedimentary rocks, made by slow deposits beneath large bodies of water; and metamorphic, meaning changed in character, typically sedimentary rocks that have passed millions of years

underground at high pressure before once again emerging at the Earth's surface as the continents keep on moving. Your handful of dirt may well contain examples of all three types of rocks, or it may consist of a single form, such as the limestones and sandstones typical of sedimentary rocks, or the granite from Vermont or the Sierra Madre mountains, excellent representatives of igneous rock.

Even more fundamental than these three types, so far as the history of rocks goes, is the fact that the motions of Earth's crustal plates has completely buried all rocks from its earliest epochs. One thing that you do *not* hold in your handful of dirt is even a tiny pebble or grain of sand that formed within the Earth's first few hundred million years, and has persisted unchanged since that time. With hard labor, geologists have found a very few regions on Earth, most notably in one corner of Greenland, with rocks as old as 3.8 billion years, 800 million years younger than the planet itself. These rocks are highly exceptional in their ages. Finding a rock older than a billion years—less than one-quarter of the Earth's age—poses a serious challenge to a beginning geologist, simply because the plates of the Earth's crust keep moving, smashing and burying rocks as one plate runs over another. For example, a few hundred million years ago, the crustal plate that carries India met the larger plates of Eurasia. As the former plowed under the latter, it raised the Himalayan Mountains—and buried a host of rocks, which themselves must have already undergone significant alteration arising from previous motions of the crust.

For those of us who seek to expand our horizons by uncovering the early history of the solar system, Earth's total lack of the earliest rocks poses a severe handicap. A geologist can hold dirt in her hand from all over the Earth, but will never have a sample of our planet's original material. In contrast, the moonlight that shines upon her reflects in large part from rocks made more than four billion years ago. If you seriously want to find the most ancient rocks of the solar system, therefore, you might plan a trip to the moon, or to Mars, where four-billion-year-old rocks presumably litter the plains. But you can do still better at advancing backward in time right here on Earth—if you know how to catch a falling star (see page 154).

Activity Two:
Consider How the Stars Made the Elements

If we look beyond the history of planet Earth, peering into space to examine the cosmic objects that surround us, we may rightly ask, as our ancestors often did, "What sort of matter are they?"

THE ELEMENTS THAT DOMINATE THE EARTH AND LIFE ITSELF

Take a look at your home, your office, your family, friends, and colleagues, and the great outdoors, and ask yourself, "What elements compose this world in which I live?" The answer carries a pleasant symmetry and simplicity. Just four elements—oxygen, silicon, aluminum, and iron—compose nearly 90 percent of the Earth's crust. When silicon combines with oxygen, these two elements form silicates, the most abundant type of rock. We tend to think of oxygen in its gaseous form, present in every breath we inhale, but far more oxygen in our immediate environment resides in silicate rocks than in the air we breathe.

Take a rock, just about any rock, and examine the hardest part of it. The majority of what you are looking at is silicon and oxygen. We have learned how to make compounds of silicon and oxygen (and other elements) in a wide variety of forms, including plastics of all types. The other two most abundant elements, iron and aluminum, are more difficult to spot in their natural form, but have proven tremendously useful to everyday life. There are two ways to look for iron in your rock. Iron appears in gold-colored flecks of iron pyrite, familiarly called "fool's gold" because it can deceive amateur miners into concluding that they have struck paydirt. Iron pyrite actually looks more like gold than gold itself does in its unrefined state. Lovers of vintage films will recall the scene in *Treasure of the Sierra Madre* in which Humphrey Bogart believes that he has found gold and dances in celebration until his wise old partner, Walter Brennan, squelches his happiness by pointing out that his discovery is fool's gold. You may not be lucky enough to strike fool's gold in your own rock, but you can easily spot iron in rocks by looking for rust-colored streaks. If you visit the Grand Canyon, or examine a photo of it, you can admire a brilliant landscape made of complex types of iron-rich rocks. These rocks are rust-colored because they are literally rusting away: their iron is slowly combining with the oxygen in the atmosphere to form new compounds. Because iron is so useful to humanity (it forms the bulk of steel), we have gone to considerable efforts to mine iron-rich rocks and extract the iron from them.

With silicon, oxygen, and iron, you have looked at three of the four most common elements near the Earth's surface. The fourth, aluminum, you will see but not recognize because aluminum appears in such variety of complex compounds that it takes a skilled amateur or a trained geologist to recognize them. Take a stroll through your kitchen, however, and you will find an abundance of aluminum products, from pots and pans to the ubiquitous aluminum foil with so many uses. Aluminum is far more difficult to extract in a relatively pure form from the soil than iron, which is why the extra effort to recycle aluminum cans and foil proves worthwhile. The four next most abundant elements on and near the Earth's surface—calcium, sodium, potassium, and magnesium—appear less frequently in manmade products, although magnesium provides an important hardening component in steel.

In contrast to the elements that form the raw materials found on and near the Earth's surface, life on Earth consists mainly of a quite different set of elements. The four most abundant elements in all living creatures are hydrogen, oxygen, carbon, and nitrogen. Only one of the four elements, oxygen, appears in both short lists. Life's elemental composition clearly implies either that life arose somewhere other than the surface of Earth—that is, within an environment rich in the elements from which life has assembled itself—or that the chemical reactions involving hydrogen, carbon, oxygen, and nitrogen proved so advantageous for the origin and evolution of life that we now find all living organisms made mainly of those four elements, even though three of them (hydrogen, carbon, and nitrogen) appear well down the list of the most abundant elements that comprise our planet Earth. Nitrogen does, however form the dominant constituent of our atmosphere, which also contains considerable amounts of carbon in the form of carbon dioxide, and hydrogen is abundant in water, which covers much of the Earth's surface (though it barely exists in the bulk of our planet).

When we look to the stars, we find that six elements dominate their composition: hydrogen, helium, oxygen, carbon, neon, and nitrogen. Helium and neon are inert gases, which stubbornly refuse to combine with any other atoms except under highly unusual conditions. The other four in the list of six—hydrogen, oxygen, carbon, and nitrogen—are precisely the four most abundant elements in living organisms on Earth! This might argue for the conclusion that life began in stars, and only later spread to planets such as our own. Against this conclusion lies the fact that stars have temperatures of many thousand degrees, even at their coolest points, and that these high temperatures prevent atoms from combining into any but the smallest and simplest molecules, such as carbon monoxide and carbon dioxide. Thus, stellar surfaces seem poor places for the formation of complex molecules, the sort that can carry the complex information embodied in all living systems. Experts far more strongly favor the conclusion that although life does consist basically of star-stuff rather than Earth-stuff, nevertheless life began, or at least underwent all but its earliest evolution, right here on Earth. In this analysis, the reason that life consists mainly of hydrogen, oxygen, carbon, and nitrogen rests on the fact that under terrestrial conditions, these atomic elements can produce complex molecules far more easily than, for example, atoms of silicon, aluminum, and iron. In other words, complex chemistry requires the elements most abundant in the stars, even if these elements, with the exception of oxygen, prove relatively under-abundant on Earth.

WHY DOES EARTH'S COMPOSITION DIFFER SO RADICALLY FROM THE SUN'S?

In analyzing the elements that form the bulk of the stars, the Earth, and ourselves, we are naturally led to ask, "Why does the Earth consist of such a different mixture of elements than the stars do? If the Earth and the other planets formed along with the sun, why don't they, like the sun, consist mainly of hydrogen, helium, oxygen, carbon, neon, and nitrogen?" The answer proves to be simple, once we recognize our Earth-chauvinistic side: the largest planets in the solar system—Jupiter, Saturn, Uranus, and Neptune—are indeed made from the same material as the sun. Jupiter and Saturn, the two largest and most massive of the sun's planets, have a composition dominated by hydrogen and helium, followed in turn, like the sun's list of most abundant elements, by oxygen, carbon, neon, and nitrogen.

The sun's four inner planets—Mercury, Venus, Earth, and Mars—formed much closer to the sun, whose heat caused the two lightest elements, hydrogen and helium, to evaporate as the planets began to form. Because neon remained stubbornly gaseous, it too has evaporated except for small pockets trapped in underground reservoirs. Much the same happened to the bulk of the nitrogen and carbon, which form solids much more reluctantly than silicon, oxygen, aluminum, iron, and magnesium do. In short, solar heating denied the sun's inner planets the chance to be gaseous and liquid, like the four large outer planets; instead, the inner planets could form only as solid objects, with a thin shell of atmospheric gases (almost none in the case of small, hot Mercury) retained by the planets' modest gravitational forces. The elements best at making solids dominate the composition of the Earth's crust and interior. Taken as a whole, our planet consists mainly of oxygen, iron, silicon, and magnesium—just what one would expect from a mixture of the most abundant elements in the sun, heated to temperatures like those on Earth today.

Why doesn't the sun's heating drive the hydrogen, helium, neon, and other gases away from the *sun*? Gravity provides the answer and the force. If you assemble an object with roughly 330,000 times the mass of Earth, you will find that it exerts such enormous gravitational forces that gases cannot escape, even when heated to temperatures of tens of thousands of degrees or more. The sun retains, to a high degree of accuracy, the same elemental composition as the matter from which it formed, four and a half billion years ago.

Among the elements heavier than hydrogen and helium, we may distinguish two categories. The elements up to and including iron, cobalt, and nickel formed by nuclear fusion during the normal lifetimes of stars. All the elements heavier than these, however, including silver, gold, tungsten, platinum, uranium, and lead, did not arise in these "ordinary" nuclear fusion processes. Normal stars never make the elements heavier than iron, nickel, and cobalt, because

NUCLEAR TRANSFORMATION INSIDE STARS

What made these elements, the marvelous assortment of atomic types that produces such variety in our lives? The history of the evolution of the elements, of how the cosmos turned one type of element into another, has become a nearly open book to astronomers and cosmologists. In the pages of this book, which humans have written during the past half-century, we may now recognize two broad categories of elements. Throughout the universe, the nuclear fusion of elementary particles made the two most abundant elements, hydrogen and helium, during the first few minutes after the big bang. However, because the universe underwent rapid expansion and cooling, this nuclear fusion produced only insignificant amounts of all the elements heavier than helium. These heavier elements formed later on, by nuclear fusion within individual stars. The stars have expelled some of these elements into space either during their late stages of evolution, called their red-giant phases, when the stars swelled to enormous sizes and ejected streams of particles at relatively modest velocities into space, or else during the violent outbursts of entire stars, called supernova explosions.

forming these elements through nuclear fusion does not release kinetic energy, as the fusion of lighter nuclei does. Instead, to fuse iron, nickel, or cobalt into heavier nuclei requires additional energy. As a result, this sort of nuclear fusion is of no "use" to a star, and therefore does not occur unless conditions become extremely strange.

Such conditions arise when a star undergoes the titanic outburst of a supernova explosion. Most stars do not explode. Instead they quietly fade away, once they have passed through their red-giant stages, as slowly cooling white dwarfs, the former cores of once-active stars, exposed after the outer layers of a red giant slowly evaporate into space, taking with them star-made elements such as carbon, nitrogen, oxygen, and neon. This fate lies in store for our sun, about five billion years in the future, when politicians will confront, and doubtless explain, the ultimate energy crisis on Earth. Less than 1 percent of all stars undergo supernova outbursts, but these explosions are responsible for all the production of the heaviest elements.

Thus, the hydrogen that forms a basic component of the Earth's oceans (but only a tiny portion of the entire Earth) came out of the big bang, whereas the medium-heavy elements that form the world and ourselves—the carbon, nitrogen, oxygen, silicon, aluminum, magnesium, and iron that dominate our biological and technological lives—arose millions or billions of years later, made inside nuclear-fusing stars and wafted into space as some of these stars approached the ends of their lives. (Because high-mass stars evolve more rapidly than low-mass stars do, these fast livers and fast diers must have had considerably more mass than our sun does.) The long spans of time available for nuclear fusion within these stars has considerably enriched the cosmos in medium-heavy elements, though they still total no more than 1 percent of the mass that resides in hydrogen and helium. In contrast, each supernova explosion provides only about one *second* within which nuclear fusion can produce elements heavier than iron, nickel, and cobalt. The gold in your wedding ring, the silver in family heirlooms, the tungsten in lamp filaments, and the uranium with which we produce electricity all owe their existence to stars that exploded more than four and a half billion years ago, mulching the cosmos with their debris, some of which ended up in our planet. The reason that you pay the big bucks for the elements heavier than iron, nickel, and cobalt resides in their scarcity, which in turn arises from the short intervals of time available to form them during supernova explosions. (Of course, scarcity can arise for other reasons, such as the exceptional pressures needed to produce diamonds from otherwise cheap carbon.)

CAN WE SEE SUPERNOVA EXPLOSIONS?

Of all astronomical activities, observing a supernova sufficiently close to the solar system to be seen without optical aid ranks among the rarest—until it occurs, whereupon everyone on Earth can participate. Supernova outbursts produce such enormous outflows of life that an exploding star anywhere in the Milky Way should be visible as a naked-eye object for several weeks. The exceptions to this rule are supernovae that lie in directions that are heavily shrouded by interstellar dust, which concentrates toward the central plane of our galaxy, just as the supernovae themselves do.

Because a supernova explosion occurs within a large spiral galaxy such as the Milky Way about once each century, we might well expect the next one soon. Not a single supernova in our galaxy has been seen since the year 1604! Small-number statistics produce seeming oddities, so although we may pronounce ourselves "overdue" for a supernova, we may nevertheless wait a century or even more for the next. Perhaps in recompense, more than one supernova can appear within a single lifetime. The supernova of 1604 followed the supernova of 1572 by only thirty-two years, so luck was in for the few astronomers with careers in the sixteenth century. (Among the most famous of these, Tycho Brahe, the chief observer of the supernova of 1572, died in 1601, whereas his one-time assistant, Johannes Kepler, the chief observer of the supernova of 1604, was born only in 1571 and therefore missed the first event in an astronomically meaningful sense.)

Indeed, since the average supernova that appears in the Milky Way has a distance greater than ten thousand light years, we may find ourselves frustrated by the thought—almost surely the fact—that dozens or even hundreds of supernovae have already exploded within our galaxy, at distances too great for their light yet to have reached us. Someday, or some year soon, we should discover which directions in the sky have supernova light on its way to us, but not yet here. Stand outside tonight and gaze among the stars to see whether you can see a new one tonight, as Tycho Brahe did one evening in 1572. Like Tycho, you must have a good acquaintance with the constellations to notice a supernova's appearance, but if it should happen that you are the first to notice a new star, and if you succeed in getting to the news media before someone else scoops you, you will have your place in the history of astronomical discovery.

DO SUPERNOVA EXPLOSIONS POSE A DANGER TO EARTH?

What would happen if a star exploded relatively close to the solar system, shooting matter outward at nearly the speed of light in such quantities that we found our planet under bombardment? Could a single nearby supernova change the course of life on Earth, or even end it?

Calculations show immediately that a truly nearby supernova would in fact present us with a catastrophe, a disaster so violent that no one would live to tell about it. If any of the thousand stars closest to the sun, for example, underwent a supernova explosion, Earth would receive a blast of cosmic-ray particles sufficient to damage or destroy all life on Earth. The thousand closest stars all lie within fifty light years from the solar system, less than ⅟₅₀₀ of the average distance to a random star in the Milky Way. In these greater dis-

tances lies our safety. In every group of a billion stars, a supernova occurs about once every ten thousand years. Reduce this number to a million, and we must wait a thousand times longer, or 10 million years, for a supernova. Take it down to a thousand, and the wait time grows to 10 billion years, the age of the Milky Way. We can live with these odds: if life on Earth lasts as long as the sun, that is, for another five billion years, the odds are better than even that no supernova will explode among the thousand closest stars during all that time.

The cosmos thus suggests that we relax and keep looking at the night skies, waiting for the sudden appearance of a super new star, shining as brightly as Sirius for a few weeks of glory. Ancient Chinese documents record more than a dozen such events, most of which went unnoticed, or at least unrecorded, in more primitive societies around the world. If you would like to explain the star of Bethlehem as a supernova, you must confront the fact that at that time, active historians recorded the great occurrences of the era, but no sources other than the New Testament noted any new bright star in the east. (By the way, you now know quite enough astronomy to realize that no star seen in the east remains in the east; instead, any such star will rise to its greatest altitude as it crosses the north-south line that passes through the zenith, then sink toward the western horizon.) We can honor supernovae quite sufficiently by celebrating the fact that they made much of our planet and ourselves, and that their outflows of cosmic-ray particles have continued to affect the evolution of life on Earth.

Activity Three:
Check the Cosmic Rainfall

The processes that built the Earth have continued, though on a sharply reduced scale of activity, to add to it throughout the past four and a half billion years. During the first few hundred million years after our planet formed, a cosmic rain of fire and ice continuously struck the Earth and the other planets in the inner solar system. This "rain" consisted of cometlike objects—dirty, frozen snowballs as large as several miles across—as well as rocky and metallic projectiles, the stuff from which our planet had been made during the previous epoch of solar-system history. The late-arriving comets may have furnished Earth with most of its oceans and atmosphere, which consist primarily of hydrogen, oxygen, and nitrogen. Because these light elements are easily vaporized, most of them escaped when the early Earth was hot, and we were fortunate in retrospect for the late rain of icy comets, which cooled things off.

Earth's atmosphere provided, as it still does, a protective shield against the smallest of the rocky and metallic objects, called meteoroids, that orbit around the sun, colliding with Earth whenever the Earth's orbit happens to intersect a meteoroid's orbit. In these collisions, the meteoroid, typically moving at speeds of five to forty miles per *second* with respect to the Earth, first encounters the Earth's atmosphere, which it attempts to push out of its way. Because the meteoroid has such an enormous velocity, the atmospheric gases cannot move as quickly as the meteoroid pushes through them, so they pile up in front of the incoming projectile, creating a tremendous heating effect that vaporizes the outer layers of the meteoroid. This vaporization produces a meteor or "shooting star," the glow of material heated to thousands of degrees, that we can see for a few seconds high above us in the atmosphere.

The Greek word "meteor" means "wind," evidence of the confusion that once existed concerning the processes that make a shooting star. Today we know that the bright streaks of light visible in the night skies are neither stars nor winds. Instead, a typical shooting star is an object with the size of a tiny pebble or a large grain of sand, weighing less than an ounce, that heats itself into momentary, glowing visibility as it plows through thin air, thirty to fifty miles above the Earth's surface, while traveling at many miles per second. Thus, if you see a meteor that takes a full second to cross part of your field of view before disappearing, it must have traveled many miles in that time—clear proof that it must be dozens of miles above you, even though it may seem to have an altitude of less than a mile.

HOW TO SEE SHOOTING STARS

You can see meteors on any clear, moonless night, but to see them well, you must decamp from the city and look at the sky in country darkness. Provide yourself with warm clothes and a good blanket, or perhaps a folding chair, then lean back and stare at the sky with a relaxed yet vigilant gaze.

Within a very few minutes, you should see at least one shooting star. If you engage in this effort in company, remember one key rule about observing meteors: except for the very brightest, every shooting star will disappear during the time that you say the words "Look over there!" As a result, calling your friends' attention to shooting stars amounts to boastfulness about the past rather than helpfulness with the present.

METEOR SHOWERS

Every day, billions of meteoroids strike the Earth, though most of them have such small masses that these objects collectively carry only about one ton of material toward our planet. In every twenty-four-hour interval, the largest of these meteoroids produce about ten million shooting stars visible in the night skies somewhere around the Earth. The fact that you can see only those meteors that happen to strike the particular patch of sky directly above you strongly limits the number of shooting stars that you can see. If you watch, far from city lights, all through an average moonless night, you might record several hundred meteors.

LOOKING FOR METEORS BEFORE OR AFTER MIDNIGHT

The frequency of shooting stars rises after midnight at any particular location, not because it has grown darker but because at times after midnight you are standing on a part of Earth that will meet incoming objects head-on. Before midnight, meteoroids must overtake your location to collide with Earth. Head-on collisions produce impacts with higher velocities than the overtaking ones do, and therefore a brighter glow from objects with the same sizes.

The brightest shooting stars, called "fireballs," appear when an object as large as a book enters the atmosphere above you. In this case, the meteor will flash just as rapidly (and far more brightly) across the sky, but even after it disappears a fuzzy bright trail will mark its passage, sometimes remaining visible for as long as a minute or two as it dissipates. Quite often, those who see a bright fireball report hearing a loud noise, but here their senses may deceive them. No object appearing dozens of miles high produces sounds we can hear simultaneously; instead, the human nervous system could insist that any object so bright as a fireball *must* be accompanied by a short, loud sound.

Some nights of the year, however, are far from average, and offer the chance to see a particularly large number of meteors. What makes these nights different from others? Meteoroids orbit the sun along a host of different trajectories, some of which contain more objects than the others. When the Earth's orbit inter-

This photograph shows a meteor or "shooting star" as it streaks away from the constellation Gemini toward the western horizon.

sects one of these trajectories rich in meteoroids, a notably increased number of objects strike the Earth each second. Astronomers call an orbit rich in meteoroids a "swarm," and the nights on which we intersect a swarm's orbit typically produce a "meteor shower," during which, with luck and a dark moonless sky, you may see more meteors after midnight than you can easily record. Year after year, the Earth meets these swarms of meteoroids, so the dates of meteor showers dot the calendar with astronomical regularity.

Each meteor shower consists of shooting stars that originate from a particular location on the sky, called the "radiant" of the meteor shower, which marks the direction toward the point where the meteor swarm's orbit crosses the Earth's. Because we mark locations on the sky with constellations and particular stars within constellations, the showers have names such as the "Leonids" and the "Perseids," whose radiants lie in the constellations Leo and Perseus, respectively. The table below provides the dates of the best meteor showers. For a typical shower, the night before and the night after the date listed in the table may bring meteors almost as good as those on the date itself.

Chapter 7 describes how to find the constellations that contain the radiants of these meteor showers other than Ursa Major (the Great Bear, which includes the Big Dipper), Orion, and Gemini, which we met in Chapters 4 and 5. Note that late July and early August are particularly fine times to look for meteors, culminating in the famous Perseid meteor shower, which in most years provides the finest display of shooting stars. In August, Perseus rides high in the sky and passes nearly overhead a few hours after midnight. If you go observing on a clear night during the second week of August, you can hope to identify this constellation by its shooting stars!

HOW MUCH DANGER LURKS IN THE SHOOTING STARS?

Even a meteoroid bright enough to produce a fireball will typically vaporize completely, leaving nothing to make an impact with the Earth's surface. Still larger objects, however, with the size of a chair, a desk, or an automobile, will survive their airy passages, though with reduced sizes and masses, to strike our planet while traveling at dozens of miles per second. The objects that do reach Earth's surface, called meteorites,

PRINCIPAL METEOR SHOWERS DURING THE YEAR

DATE OF PEAK ACTIVITY	NAME OF METEOR SHOWER	CONSTELLATION OF RADIANT
January 3	Quadrantids	Bootes/Draco border*
April 22	Lyrids	Lyra
May 6	Eta Aquarids	Aquarius
July 28	Delta Aquarids	Aquarius
August 1	Capricornids	Capricorn
August 11	Perseids	Perseus
October 21	Orionids	Orion
November 5	Northern Taurids	Taurus
November 12	Southern Taurids	Taurus
November 17	Leonids	Leo
December 14	Geminids	Gemini
December 23	Ursids	Ursa Major*

Notes: The Quadrantid meteor shower, which was named after an old constellation, now merged into its neighbors, has its radiant point at the northern end of the constellation Bootes, where the Herdsman encounters the faint stars of Draco, the Dragon. Ursa Major is, of course, the Great Bear, whose brightest stars form the Big Dipper.

provide scientists with an opportunity to examine the oldest, least altered material in the solar system. Some meteorites consist of matter that condensed into solid form four and a half billion years ago, and has done nothing but orbit the sun since then. To be sure, its fiery passage through the atmosphere must have changed the meteorite's outermost crust considerably, but its interior offers nearly pristine matter from the earliest epochs, soon after the sun and its planets had begun to form.

Those who fear rather than admire the possibilities of meteoritic impacts can take comfort from the fact that recorded history, though admittedly incomplete, includes only one person hit by a meteorite (a woman living in a trailer in Alabama, apparently struck on the first bounce by a meteorite that came through her ceiling) and one animal fatality (a dog killed in Egypt). Furthermore, since the victim acquires title to the impactor by all moral and international law, meteorite impacts have an upside: collectors will pay large amounts for anything so rare as a stone from heaven that actually struck a person. On October 9, 1992, a bright fireball appeared over West Virginia and Pennsylvania, where it broke into several fragments, the largest of which weighed twenty-seven pounds when it struck a parked car (a 1980 Chevrolet Malibu) near Peekskill, New York. Not only the stony meteorite but the car as well fetched high prices on the open market for Earth-impacting objects. The market has opened considerably wider since then, thanks to the advent of computer-based auctions, on which you will find hundreds of meteorites listed for sale, so that you can buy a piece of a rock from outer space for only a few dollars. During the 1890s, Robert E. Peary, who later claimed to be the first person to reach the North Pole, brought three large pieces of an iron-rich meteorite from Cape York, Greenland to New York City, where he sold them to the American Museum of Natural History for the then-enormous sum of $40,000. The largest of these pieces, still on display at the Rose Planetarium in New York, weighs thirty-four tons.

On short time scales, we can safely pronounce the Earth almost free of death threats from meteorite impacts. Nevertheless, we can also calculate that on the average, about two hundred people die each year from these impacts. How is this possible, if no one has yet been reported killed by a stone falling from space? The answer lies in the long time scale: every 30 million years or so, we all die, and 6 billion people (Earth's present population) divided by 30 million years gives two hundred deaths per year!

Can this really be true? Apparently so. The past two decades have seen great progress in our ability to determine when large objects have struck the Earth with devastating consequences. Because small objects are extremely abundant, medium-sized objects somewhat common, and large objects rare, we can easily see why huge impacts occur far less often than small ones do. By far the best-known large impact on Earth occurred at the end of the Cretaceous era, 65 million years ago, when an object about ten miles across struck the Yucatán peninsula, producing a crater more than a hundred miles across, which exists today (partly beneath the Gulf of Mexico) in a highly eroded state. Because this impact coincides in time with the sudden demise of all dinosaurs, as well as of many other species of animal and planet life, scientists conclude (with some dissenters) that this "mass extinction" arose as the result of the impact, which must have flung dust and grit high above the Earth's

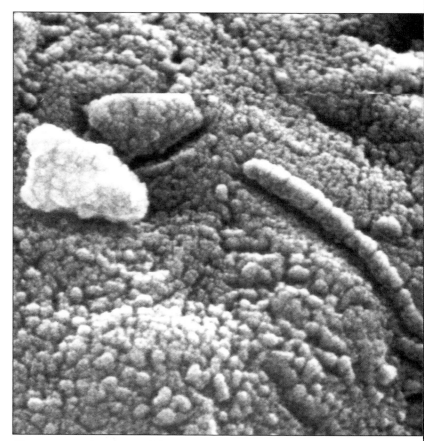

The most stunning aspect of the meteorite found in Antarctica in 1984 consists of these tubular and ovoid structures, no more than one-millionth of a meter long, that resemble fossils of tiny organisms on Earth.

atmosphere, through the ten-mile-wide hole that the impacting object made. As the dust slowly settled back to the surface, a months-long darkness lay over the land, apparently sufficient to kill all dinosaurs. This opened a host of ecological niches for our shrewlike mammalian ancestors, which for more than a hundred million years had scurried through the forests, easy prey for the dinosaurs that ruled the Earth, yet capable of surviving, though doubtless in reduced numbers, the catastrophe that ended the long reign of their reptilian overlords.

Other mass extinctions punctuate the fossil record of life on Earth at roughly thirty-million-year intervals, including the Permian-Triassic extinction nearly 250 million years ago, which apparently killed almost 90 percent of all species, and thus came close to wiping out life entirely on our planet. The most recent of these, the Miocene extinction about 11 million years in the past, did nothing so spectacular as its dinosaur-killing predecessor, but nevertheless qualifies in the list. And what of its successor? When can we expect the next mass extinction to occur, when once again an object roughly 10 miles across strikes the Earth?

On a probabilistic basis, the answer must be: cosmically soon, in no more than 20 to 40 million years, perhaps as soon as 10 million years from now, perhaps in a century or less. From a selfish, human point of view, we draw a considerable distinction between a life-removing impact that will occur in 10 million years and one that may occur before the twenty-first century has run its course. The former possibility offers later generations—much later!—the chance to deal with the threat of an onrushing object, an asteroid or comet as large as the District of Columbia, which might be diverted or blown apart before it could strike the Earth. The latter inspires fear and movies, as well as a governmental effort, called Project Spaceguard, to locate and to catalogue all objects larger than a mile or so whose orbits might carry them directly into the path of our planet as we calmly orbit the sun. Despite its name, Project Spaceguard currently aims no farther than producing this catalogue. Deciding what to do in the event that we find objects that pose a serious threat to Earth must await, as other crucial decisions do, the calm consideration of a benevolent, democratically elected government.

Just under a century ago, in June 1908, a fireball appeared over the Tunguska region of Siberia. This object was apparently a comet with a diameter of only a few hundred yards that exploded from its sudden heating high above the Earth's surface, producing a blast wave that felled trees for dozens of miles but, in that remote area, resulted in no known fatalities. If we face only similar objects, or even somewhat larger ones, such as the object that produced the mile-wide Meteor Crater in Arizona some fifty thousand years ago, we can be confident that life will survive easily, no matter what local disasters may occur. It is the objects more than a couple of miles across that pose life-threatening dangers to all of humanity, so we do well to keep our eyes open, and even to debate what we should do if we find one whose orbit will cross our own.

MEDITATION

What chance exists for "cosmic recycling," the transformation of the more complex elements back into simpler ones? For this, we would require that the expansion of the universe reverse itself, billions of years in the future, so that all of space began to shrink, bringing cosmic objects closer and closer, until finally, in a mighty "big crunch," the universe once again became an arena of near-infinite density, where nuclear reactions broke apart all the nuclei so

The famous Meteor Crater near Flagstaff, Arizona, spans nearly a mile and was created about 50,000 years ago when an object the size of a house slammed into the desert terrain.

laboriously manufactured during the immense span of time since the big bang that began the universe in its current state of expansion. Astronomers once considered that a "big crunch" might well occur, about one hundred billion years from now, and might indeed lead to cosmic recycling, as a new big bang arose from the ashes of the old.

Recent news from the cosmological front has radically altered astronomers' concepts of the universal future. By discovering that a class of exploding stars called "Type Ia supernovae" all rise to nearly the same maximum luminosity in their light output, astronomers have acquired, as they have long desired, a reliable "standard candle," a set of objects that all have the same luminosity or true brightness. The comparison of apparent brightnesses for these objects provides the ratios of the objects' distances: if one object with the same luminosity as another appears only one-quarter as bright, the fainter object must lie twice as far away. The objects' distances in turn can be correlated with the speeds with which they are receding from us, revealed in their spectra of light. Every model of the cosmos that describes its past, present, and future expansion predicts a unique relationship between the distances and recession velocities of objects seen at different distances, and thus as they were at different times in the past.

Using the Type Ia supernovae as their standard candles, astronomers have reached a startling conclusion: instead of slowing its expansion, as expected from the mutual gravitational attraction among all the objects in the cosmos, the universe has been *accelerating*, expanding at an increasing rate during the past few billion years! These results, still subject to the scrutiny of scientific skepticism, imply that the universe will never cease expanding and start contracting. Instead, the cosmos will expand ever more rapidly, so that many billions of years from now, not only will all the stars have burned themselves out, but those stellar corpses will also find themselves at immense distances from one another, as the universe rushes vacuously onward toward near-emptiness and total darkness.

What could make the cosmos accelerate its expansion, despite gravity's tendency to slow it down? The only reasonable answer (though "reasonable" has a flexible meaning here) points to the "cosmological constant" that Albert Einstein introduced into his equations describing the overall behavior of the universe. Einstein pointed out that these equations must include a constant of unknown value; in 1918, when no one knew of the universe's expansion, he suggested a value that would keep the universe in a static state, neither expanding nor contracting. After Edwin Hubble had discovered the expansion of the universe, Einstein pronounced this constant his "greatest blunder," and concluded that its value should be zero. But the recent observations imply a non-zero value—not the one Einstein once plumped for, but another one entirely, one that corresponds to the observed relationship between the distances and recession velocities of the Type Ia supernovae. This value implies that every cubic centimeter of empty space actually teems with "dark energy," energy undetectable by ordinary means but entirely real, visible only in its effects on the expansion of the universe. Since no good explanation of this dark energy now exists, we should maintain a skeptical outlook, but if the observations receive further validation, it may well be time to conclude that the cosmic expansion will not only continue forever but will accelerate toward an empty and nearly meaningless future.

Should this prove to be so, we must abandon our hopes that cosmic recycling, in the form of a big crunch and a big bounce into another cycle of cosmic expansion, will eventually cancel our errors and produce a pristine new universe. The latest cosmological news implies that we had better take care of our own environment, rather than waiting for the universe to do so in about a hundred billion years' time. One more excuse for inaction thus vanishes into the dustbin of history! It is time to shape up and have a look at the Milky Way, in which we must live for the foreseeable future.

Chapter *Nine*

The Great Wheel in the Sky

A meteor or "shooting star" arises when a dust particle heats to glowing as it speeds into Earth's atmosphere. Behind it shine the stars in our Milky Way galaxy, approximately ten trillion times more distant than the meteor's few dozen miles.

Who has seen the great wheel in the sky, the milky way that runs through the heavens? Our ancestors all saw it, marveling at the milk-white path of light that ran across the dome of night. Today, we have nearly lost the milky way: the name more often evokes a candy bar than a great cosmic phenomenon. In a lopsided tradeoff, public awareness of the milky way has diminished at the same time that private knowledge, held by astronomers and by those who care about the arrangement of the cosmos, has risen. You can help to restore a better equilibrium by making sure that you can recognize and enjoy the milky way that runs around the sky.

For untold millennia on Earth, the true arrangement of the cosmos lay hidden in darkness. All who gazed at the skies could watch the heavens in their majestic rotation, with some stars rising into view while others sank in the west, all the stars twinkling (so we now know) as their beams of light passed through our ever-restless atmosphere. The planets wandered among the stars, confining their meanderings to the constellations that form the zodiac, shining with a steadier light than that from the stars. The moon, likewise limited to the zodiac, performed its monthly tour around the dome of heaven, with small deviations from a steady, uniform motion that had no easy explanation. As the year passed, observers saw familiar stars rising progressively earlier on each successive night, while the sun, whose location against the starry background could easily be deduced by anyone with a good memory for the constellations, made its annual circle around the ecliptic, the line that marks the center of the zodiac.

THE MILK-WHITE CIRCLE IN THE SKY

In addition to the sun, moon, planets, and stars, another glow appeared in the heavens, a diffuse, whitish band of light that made a great circle around the sky. Observers noted that because this great circle has an orientation on the sky quite unlike that of the zodiac that encloses the ecliptic, part of it passed close to the north celestial pole and could therefore be seen at all seasons of the year. On the other hand, unlike the zodiac, the milky band of light exhibited no relation to the motions of the wanderers in the sky, though it did cross the zodiac in two places.

THE MANY NAMES OF THE MILKY WAY

More than two thousand years ago, the Chinese called the whitish band of light in the sky "Tien Ho," the "Celestial River." At the same time, the Jews named it "Nhar di Nur," the "River of Light," though they also knew its title in ancient Akkadia, the "Great Serpent," and apparently referred to it as such in the Book of Job with the words "By his spirit he hath garnished the heavens; his hand hath formed the crooked serpent." To many cultures, the band of light seemed a pathway in the sky, called the "Path of Aryaman" in early Hindu mythology, the "Silver Street" by the Celts, "Wotan's Way" (later "Jacob's Way") by the Germans, and the "Winter Street" in Sweden. The Hungarians named it "Hada Kuttya," meaning the Path of War, perhaps because their ancestors had followed it from central Asia. Many Native American tribes in North America, much like the Vikings, saw the band of light as the gods' pathway to the resting place of heroes killed in battle; both the Inuit and the Bushmen of Africa named it the "Ashen Path"; and the Polynesians called it the "Long, Blue, Cloud-Eating Shark."

To this pearly band of light, ancient Roman authors assigned the name "milky circle" or "milky way," the name in general use today. By employing lower-case letters for this appellation, we can distinguish the milky way, the band of light that we see in the sky, from the upper-case Milky Way galaxy, the host of stars whose light produces this band. This relationship lay hidden for centuries, until Galileo turned his first telescope toward the milky way and discovered that the milky band of light arises from a great host of individual stars. Three centuries more had to pass before astronomers finally realized that we live within a giant agglomeration of hundreds of billions of stars, shaped like a pie plate or a frisbee. Seen from within, the Milky Way therefore appears as a band of light circling the entire sky, arching almost to the north celestial pole and dipping, on its opposite side, nearly to the sky's south pole, where it shines with news just as important to astronomers but never visible to observers north of the Equator.

Activity One:
Finding the Milky Way in Modern Society

To all who admired the skies in preindustrial times, the milky way provided an integral part of the heav-ens, as evident as the stars that formed the constellations and the planets that moved through them. Today, with artificial illumination that banishes the dark of night, and a perpetual haze or worse that hangs over many of our cities, the milky way has disappeared from view for a large fraction of the world's population. Citing this fact, the August 24, 2001 *New York Times* lamented editorially that "we have lost, or are near to losing, what should be the simple, every-night awareness of the stars overhead." I now ask that you transport yourself to the darkest place you can safely get to—if you live in a city, get yourself to a rural area; if you're already in a rural area, hie yourself to the mountains or the desert and let the milky way overwhelm you. Your travels will be well rewarded when you observe the milky way shining so brilliantly that you will immediately see why our ancestors regarded it as a key component of the heavens.

OBSERVING THE MILKY WAY IN FALL AND WINTER

If you are looking for the milky way from a location in the northern hemisphere, you may conveniently divide your task, and the milky way itself, into two

This photograph of the milky way shows the brilliance of the combined light from billions of individual stars.

parts, naming them the "summer milky way" and the "milky way of fall and winter." These two segments meet in and share the constellation Cassiopeia, the region on the sky where the milky way passes closest to the north celestial pole and can therefore be seen during all months of the year.

On any fall or winter night when you can see Orion, look for the milky way between Betelgeuse, the red star in the Hunter's bright shoulder, and the feet of Gemini the Twins. You should detect the whitish band, part of which runs past Gemini's feet, without much difficulty. If you can't see this faint glow of light, you are the victim of unfavorable circumstances, typically of overbright stray light from urban illumination. To overcome this light, you must find a darker spot; be sure to let your eyes adjust to the darkness for a few minutes in order to gain their maximum sensitivity. With any luck, you will then spot the milky way, glowing with the light of millions of stars, all of them many thousand light-years away. Take a minute longer to study this glow, noting that even though (so we now know) you are seeing starlight in abundance, the light from the milky way seems notably unlike the light produced by a star. The contrast arises, in large part, from the fact that your eyes perceive individual points of light quite differently from a band of light. Nevertheless, we do see stars when we observe the milky way—the host of stars that crowd the plane of our flattened galaxy, so that since we inhabit that plane, we encounter a multitude of stars in whatever direction along that plane we look. These stars paint the sky white with their combined output of light.

Once you have the milky way well identified, you can trace it outward from Orion in two opposite directions around the sky. First, look toward the east and south of Orion to see the milky way splashing through the region between Procyon in the Little Dog and Sirius in the Big Dog. Look still farther to the south and east, past the Big Dog, to encounter the regions of the sky just above the southern horizon on a clear dark night in the fall, and you may be able to see the milky way in Puppis, the Ship's Stern.

Now look for the milky way in the opposite direction, northward from Orion. There you will see the milky path as it runs through the part of Taurus directly north of Orion's shoulders, then into Auriga, where it passes to the south of the constellation's brightest star, Capella. The band of light then continues to the north and west,

where it runs through the center of Perseus. This constellation, held to represent one of the great heroes of Greek and Roman mythology, contains a number of medium-bright stars, which stubbornly refuse to look anything like a hero or even an ordinary man; at best they seem to fall into a straggly line reminiscent of a crocodile. In some compensation for this constellational lack of correspondence with mythology, the milky way shines more brightly in Perseus than it does in Auriga, Gemini, or Orion. The brightness continues as you move your gaze through Perseus still farther toward the north celestial pole, where you encounter the next milky way constellation, Cassiopeia.

Cassiopeia, taken to represent a queen seated on her throne, contains seven stars about as bright as those in Perseus, but grouped more tightly and into an easily recognizable form. Cassiopeia's shape resembles that of a queen's high-backed chair, though it can be better imagined as the letter W with sprawling, imperfect sides (or as an equally splayed M at the times when Cassiopeia's position in the sky turns the W upside down). Cassiopeia and the Big Dipper occupy regions of the sky that lie in opposite directions from the north celestial pole. As a result, during the late spring and early summer, when the Big Dipper rides high in the sky and almost reaches the overhead point as seen from latitudes in the mid–United States, Cassiopeia dips close to the horizon. Six months later, during the late fall and early winter, it is Cassiopeia that rises highest in the sky, while the Big Dipper nearly grazes the northern horizon.

Take a moment, then, to admire the great sweep of the milky way, from Cassiopeia at its northernmost down through Perseus and Auriga, then through the regions of the sky between Gemini and Orion, onward between Canis Major and Canis Minor, and so downward into the southern horizon. You can easily perceive that if the Earth were transparent, you would see the milky way continue on its way through the parts of the sky that never rise, until, having reached its southernmost point in the sky, it would turn north again to become the milky way that we see in summertime.

FINDING THE MILKY WAY IN SUMMER

During the summer and early fall, you can easily see the portion of the milky way that runs southward from Cassiopeia toward and through the Summer Triangle (see page 131). The milky band of light shines particularly brightly in Cygnus, where it passes directly along the body of the Swan, and in Aquila, the constellation to the south of Cygnus, where it likewise coincides with the Eagle's fuselage. If you look closely at the milky way in Cygnus, in the area between Cygnus and Aquila, and in Aquila itself, you will see that the milky way seems to divide, with dark lanes within the whitish band that marks out a great circle around the sky. Your eyes and brain will insist that here you can see *through* the milky way out to greater distances, when in fact the reverse phenomenon occurs: obscuring clouds of dust block the light from those portions of the milky way, so your line of sight ends at a *shorter* distance from the Earth when you look at the dark lanes than it does when you observe the bright milky way.

To the south of Aquila, the milky way grows a bit dimmer as it runs through the small and faint constellation called Scutum, the Shield; it then brightens again, and also widens, as it passes through Sagittarius and Scorpius. As we mentioned in Chapter 7, the boundary between these two constellations marks one of the two regions on the sky where the milky way intersects the zodiac. The other, exactly opposite this one on the sky, lies at the boundary between Taurus and Gemini, where once again the zodiac and the milky way, the two great wheels around the sky, cross one another. Because the Sagittarius-Scorpius boundary lies in the direction of center of the Milky Way galaxy, here we find the sky particularly rich in star clusters. This direction toward the

The three constellations of the Summer Triangle include Lyra, at the top of this photograph, Cygnus, to the left, and Aguila, to the lower right.

center marks a natural anchor for inspecting the milky way, though if you sweep your gaze over about 90 degrees, from this direction back through Aquila and Cygnus to Cassiopeia, you will see that the milky way shines with nearly the same brightness from all directions, a tribute to the enormous numbers of stars that we observe in all directions around the frisbee shape we call the Milky Way.

Activity Two:
The Milky Way from the Southern Hemisphere

Those who seek the power of the sky, connecting with the cosmos by learning its bright lights and dark shadows, should not suffer the indignity of passing their lives without seeing the southern third of the dome of heaven, the portion that never rises above the horizons of observers in the United States and Europe. For astronomers who study the objects in the Milky Way galaxy, this dictum goes double, for they know that the southern milky way contains some of the finest and most intriguing objects that our galaxy offers for our delight.

To begin, you should admire the center of our galaxy, which lies in the direction of Sagittarius, close to its boundary with Scorpius. This area, which also forms part of the zodiac by cosmic accident, does rise well above northern horizons in summertime, but to nothing like the altitudes that it achieves in Chile, for example, where great observatories can study the galactic center as it passes directly overhead—a significant part of the reason for siting those observatories in the foothills of the Andes. Even farther to the south, however, lie fantastic regions in the Milky Way, including the darkest dust cloud and some of the most brilliant star-studded skies. In this activity, I invite you to travel again, if not below the equator, then as far as the nearest planetarium that, for educational and recreational purposes, will show you the parts of the sky visible only from the southern hemisphere. For once, living within an urban area offers you an advantage, since the finest planetariums are located in the largest cities. A phone call or two will locate a star show that includes the southern milky way. For the truly adventurous and fortunate, a trip to the southern hemisphere may be a real possibility. Let us take a tour down south, for the moment in our imagination, and see how the milky way looks from Australia, New Zealand, South America, or southern Africa.

THE CHIEF CONSTELLATIONS OF THE SOUTHERN HEMISPHERE

You can begin your tour with the shock of seeing familiar constellations standing on their heads. By now, as an experienced stargazer, you have learned to recognize Orion in winter and Scorpius in summer, and to use these constellations to orient yourself to find the stars nearby. When you step outside on a clear night in Sydney or Rio de Janeiro, Johannesburg or Auckland, or anywhere else south of the equator, however, you will encounter some difficulty in recognizing these familiar star groups, for they will appear to have turned themselves upside down! A moment's thought will show that the stars have remained unchanged, but that your move to the southern hemisphere has given you a new perspective with which to view the familiar star patterns.

Once you have recovered a feeling of ease with the constellations that you know, you are ready to use them to explore the skies never seen in New York or California. In fall or winter, you can start with Orion and its companion, the Big Dog, the latter of which now rises overhead and shows its full majesty, sporting the brightest of all stars plus three second-magnitude stars nearly as bright as those in Orion's belt. The milky way runs right past Orion and Canis Major, heading past the overhead point toward the south, where it enters the constellations Puppis, Vela, and Carina. These constellations, whose Latin names mean "the Stern," "the Sail," and "the Keel," respectively, form part of what was once the largest constellation, Argo the Ship, named after the mythological vessel piloted by Jason and his Argonauts. Argo barely appeared above the southern horizon for observers in southern Europe, and had been rather poorly delineated; when astronomers began their systematic mapping of the southern skies, they found it appropriate to subdivide the ship into its constituent parts.

Of course, since Argo did not look much like a ship, Puppis hardly looks like a ship's stern (not that one immediately expects a known configuration for a stern), nor does Carina look like a ship's keel. Vela does look something like a sail, but only because any group of stars has a good chance at such a resemblance, given the various forms that a sail can take as the wind varies. Instead of attempting to discriminate among these constellations, you can profitably take the following simplified approach. Look for the brightest star in Carina, namely Canopus, the second-brightest star in the sky, which lies directly south of Sirius and about 36 degrees away from it—nearly twice the size of your outstretched hand held at arm's length (see page 93 for a description of how to find Canopus with Sirius as a guide). To the east of Canopus, you will see two medium-bright stars spaced about 10 degrees apart, not quite so bright as those in the hindquarters of the Big Dog to the north. These two are the brightest stars in Vela the Sail. You can then mark out a roughly equilateral triangle whose three corners are the rear end of the Big Dog, Canopus, and the more northern of the two stars in Vela. The milky way runs through Puppis (basically invisible as a constellation), then slips through Vela, where it passes by one of the two brightest stars, the one farther from Canopus. It then slides through the part of Carina that lies even farther from Canopus and contains no bright stars, and finally, at its southernmost points, enters the two finest constellations of the deep southern skies, Crux and Centaurus.

THE SOUTHERN CROSS AND THE SOUTH CELESTIAL POLE

Crux, the Southern Cross, and Centaurus, the Centaur, are best seen during May, June, and July, when they rise highest in the sky. In the southern hemisphere, these months end the fall and begin the winter, so the stars come out fairly early, with Virgo visible toward the north and Arcturus near the northern horizon. High in the south, you will see the sky's tightest grouping of first-magnitude stars, two in Centaurus and two in the Southern Cross.

Crux's cross-like structure, much more compact than the Northern Cross in Cygnus, consists of four stars that mark the ends of its two perpendicular arms, which run almost precisely from north to south and from east to west, with the north-south arm about 50 percent longer than the east-west arm. The brightest of the four stars lies at the southern end of the north-south arm, while the second-brightest star occupies the eastern end of the east-west arm. Both of these are first-magnitude stars. The third-brightest star, at the northern point of the cross, is one of the brightest of the second-magnitude stars, so Crux nearly has three first-magnitude stars within its small area. The least

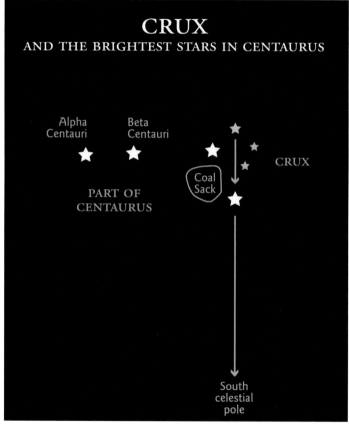

CRUX
AND THE BRIGHTEST STARS IN CENTAURUS

Alpha Centauri

Beta Centauri

CRUX

Coal Sack

PART OF CENTAURUS

South celestial pole

The four stars that form the Southern Cross are aligned almost exactly in an east-west direction for the short arm of the cross and a north-south direction for the cross's long arm.

impressive of the four stars in the cross, at the west end of the east-west arm, nevertheless shines quite brightly, as does a fifth star in the constellation, which lies nearly on the line that joins this western end to the southern, brightest tip of the cross.

The Southern Cross deserves your attention for two additional reasons. First, here the milky way appears arguably at its best, with its host of stars producing a pearly glow, along with several open star clusters easily seen with binoculars. One of these, visible with unaided eyes as well, lies close to the second-brightest star in the cross, just a bit to its southeast, that is, on the opposite side of that star from the center of the cross and in the direction toward the brightest star. Bright as the milky way is, it disappears completely in one particularly dark region, called the Coal Sack, that lies near the brightest of the four stars in the cross. Look from that star a bit to the east, in the same direction as that from the center of the cross to the second-brightest star. Within a short distance of the brightest star you should find the Coal Sack as a patch of black, outlined against a fairly bright region of the milky way. The Coal Sack is the blackest, darkest region on the sky, not because of any absence of stars in that direction but rather because of a high density of obscuring dust that blocks all the light from the stars behind.

Second, the Southern Cross plays the same role in the southern hemisphere that the Big Dipper does in the northern: you can use it to find the south celestial pole. No bright star lies near this pole, a reminder of how fortunate we are to have Polaris, the North Star, just a degree from the north celestial pole. Instead, to find the south pole of the sky, you extend the long axis of the Southern Cross from its northern tip through the brightest of the stars in the cross, the southernmost one, and continue southward for four and a half times the length of that north-south arm. There, in an unassuming patch of dark sky, lies the point directly above the Earth's south pole, around which the heavens seem to turn for any observer south of the equator. Partly for this reason, but much more for its glorious aspect, the Southern Cross appears on the flags of five countries south of the Equator: Australia, Brazil, New Zealand, Papua New Guinea, and Western Samoa. Brazil has even named its currency, the cruzeiro, after this most identifiable of all the southern constellations.

CENTAURUS AND THE CLOSEST STARS TO THE SUN

Next to Crux lies its neighbor, Centaurus the Centaur, as large a constellation as any, utterly unlike a centaur except as a melange of differing items. Centaurus spreads to the east and north of Crux, covering an area of the sky about fifteen times larger than Crux does, and contains a number of objects fascinating to astronomers, including one of the finest globular star clusters to be seen in the heavens. The modest portion of Centaurus that embraces the milky way lies immediately to the east of the Southern Cross, where the two brightest stars of the constellation shine. Both of these are first-magnitude stars, by definition ranking among the twenty brightest stars in the sky, so Crux and Centaurus between them possess four of these twenty, all located within an area of the sky smaller than the constellation Orion.

The two brightest stars in Centaurus, directly to the east of Crux, lie in a line that points directly at the second-brightest star in the Southern Cross. They therefore perform a useful service by helping you make sure that you have found the true cross. Confusion in this area can arise because a larger and fainter set of four

stars, to the north and west of Crux, at the point where Vela and Carina meet one another, also forms a cross, with its arms approximately parallel to the arms of Crux. This "False Cross" that lies to the northwest of Crux has confused many a first-time searcher for the Southern Cross. Since the False Cross has no first-magnitude stars nearby, the two bright stars in Centaurus make clear beyond a doubt that you have found the true Crux.

Of these two bright stars, the one farther from Crux, Alpha Centauri, is the third-brightest star in the sky, outshone only by Sirius and Canopus. The luck of the celestial draw has placed two of the three brightest stars in regions of the sky never visible from most of the United States and all of Europe. Alpha Centauri lies directly to the south of Arcturus, the fourth-brightest star, but fully 80 degrees away—almost one-quarter of a full circle, or nearly the full distance from the horizon up to the zenith. Like Sirius and unlike Canopus, Alpha Centauri owes its brightness to its nearness. In Alpha Centauri, we find the sun's closest neighbor stars. A telescope reveals two stars, each much like our sun in temperature and intrinsic brightness, around which orbits a much cooler, dimmer star called Proxima Centauri because it is actually (by a small amount) the closest of all stars to the sun. If all the stars in the sky were to vanish simultaneously (an event that astronomers judge no more likely than pigs flying over the North Pole), the Alpha Centauri stars would be the first to disappear from our view, only four and a half years later. To the east of Centaurus, the southern milky way passes through three or four small and unentertaining constellations before entering the familiar fishhook tail of Scorpius and crossing the boundary between the Scorpion and Sagittarius the Archer. In this region of the sky, the milky way is more recognizable than any of the stars.

FINISHING YOUR TOUR OF THE MILKY WAY

The nether regions of the milky way take us nicely through a tour of the chief constellations of the southern skies: Carina, Vela, Crux, and Centaurus. If this list seems skimpy, recall that Scorpius, Sagittarius, and Canis Major are southern constellations too, since all their stars likewise lie south of the celestial equator, though not so far to the south that we cannot see them from mid-northern latitudes. Orion, Virgo, and Aquila spread across both sides of the celestial equator, so we can easily count ten

bright southern milky-way constellations if we are in the mood to do so.

If you find yourself with the urge to count all twenty of the first-magnitude stars, you can group them by season and by your location on Earth. Capella, Aldebaran, Pollux, Betelgeuse, Rigel, Procyon, Sirius, and Regulus are stars of the late fall and winter, visible from either hemisphere because they all lie in the general vicinity of the celestial equator. In spring and summer, Arcturus and Spica, along with the three stars in the Summer Triangle, Vega, Deneb, and Altair, can likewise be seen from both hemispheres, though Vega and Arcturus rise far higher in the sky for northern-hemisphere observers. The two brightest stars in Crux, like those in Centaurus, are for southern-hemisphere observers only. So too is Canopus, the second-brightest star, which barely clears the horizon in the southern United States. We have seen how to locate these eighteen first-magnitude stars by star-hopping from constellation to constellation. The list becomes complete with two more stars, both of which lie to the south of the celestial equator. One of these, Fomalhaut, can be easily seen from the United States and Europe, whereas the other, Achernar, cannot, since it lies as far to the south as Canopus, Crux, and the two brightest stars in Centaurus.

Fomalhaut, whose name reflects the Arabic "Fum al Hut," or "Fish's Mouth," is the chief star—indeed, the only easily visible star—in the constellation Pisces Australis, the Southern Fish. This constellation lies to the south of the zodiacal constellation Pisces (the Fish, pure and simple), and can be found during the fall months by locating the western side of the Great Square of Pegasus, the side closest to the Summer Triangle, whose stars are slightly brighter than those that form the opposite, eastern side (see page 134). If you draw an imaginary line through the two stars on the western side of the Great Square, passing from the northern through the southern star, and extend it southward for three and a half times that distance, you will find Fomalhaut, seemingly alone in a large region of the sky. If you ask what might have caused the fish frenzy among constellation names, the answer turns on the fact that we are in the astrological "water" region of the sky, where Pisces, Aquarius, and Capricorn are all "water signs"; apparently plenty of water area remained to be filled, not only by Pisces Australis but also by Cetus, the Sea Monster, whose faint stars lie to the south of Pisces, which itself mostly occupies the space to the south of the eastern side of Pegasus's Great Square.

To complete your list of the twenty brightest stars in the sky of Earth, you must find Achernar, the brightest star in Eridanus, the River. As its name implies, Eridanus is another of the water constellations, located in the same general region of the sky as Pisces and Pisces Australis. Eridanus depicts a river as a long, winding stellar waterway that extends nearly to Rigel in Orion, and consists entirely of unimpressive stars—except for Achernar, which appears in the same general region of the sky as Fomalhaut, but lies so much farther to the south of the celestial equator that you cannot see it easily unless you visit the southern hemisphere. If you do, however, you will find Achernar high in the sky from October through February. Named after the Arabic "Al Ahir al Nahr," meaning "the End of the River," Achernar is the brightest star in the southern skies during those months, not counting the stars in Crux and Centaurus, which in those seasons barely clear the northern horizon. On January 4, 1922, on the bleak island of South Georgia, as far south of the equator as London is north of it, the great Antarctic explorer Ernest Shackleton penciled his last diary entry, a few hours before his fatal heart attack. "In the darkening twilight, I saw a lone star hovering gem-like above the bay," wrote Shackleton, who probably saw Achernar or the somewhat fainter Fomalhaut as his final celestial object.

Activity Three:
Looking Beyond the Milky Way

Now that you have mastered the skies of fall, winter, spring, and summer, including the twelve constellations of the zodiac, twice as many constellations that take you around the milky way, and the twenty brightest stars of the entire sky, you are ready for your graduation exercise: observing the Andromeda galaxy.

All the stars that can be seen as individual points of light with your unaided eyes, rather than as part of a star cluster or of the diffuse milky way, lie within about 1,600 light years of the solar system. The milky way's light arises collectively from millions of stars, too distant to be seen as individuals, with distances from us ranging from about five thousand to thirty thousand light years. Thus, the milky way bathes the Earth with light that arose at the dawn of civilization on this planet. But if you want to beggar these distances and light travel times, and to perceive an object so far from us that its light left when our ancestors roamed the Olduvai Gorge

The dark night sky, photographed at the Cerro Tololo Observatory in Chile, reveals the milky way (right) in all its glory. To the left of the central dome appear the Magellanic Clouds, the Milky Way's two largest satellite galaxies.

in search of edible plants, you must look far beyond the confines of the Milky Way galaxy, to the neighbor galaxies closest to our own. How far are they?

The Milky Way has two sizable satellite galaxies, the Large and Small Magellanic clouds, easy to see (and, if you are a sailor who sees them for the first time, easy to mistake for clouds). These galaxies, however, lie so close to the south celestial pole of the sky that they never appear to observers in the United States (except on a few happy nights for those who live in southern Florida). For northern-hemisphere observers, the key chance to look beyond the Milky Way resides in the great galaxy in Andromeda, a near-twin of our own giant spiral galaxy.

The Andromeda galaxy (hardly the only galaxy in that constellation, but by so much the closest and brightest that astronomers routinely call it so) has a distance of 2.2 million light years, half a million times the distance to the nearest stars, and a quarter of a million times the distance to Sirius. If we round off these large numbers, we can say that if you look at the closest stars in the Milky Way and at the Andromeda galaxy, you are using your eyes to record the light from stars at distances that differ by a factor comparable to *one million*. It is worth emphasizing this fact as a reminder that even though all distances in astronomy are enormous, some are far more enormous than others. Sirius, about 50 trillion miles from Earth, is a million times more distant than Venus or Mars when those planets are close to Earth, and almost a quarter of a billion times farther from us than our moon. The Andromeda galaxy, 250,000 times farther away than Sirius, has a distance of 13 million trillion miles, more than 50 trillion times the distance to the moon— which itself lies so far from Earth, nearly a quarter of a million miles, that only a few humans have made the journey to our planet's satellite.

Astronomers love these immense numbers, even though they know that to the public they all seem much the same. Since we are completing a tour of the cosmos accessible to our immediate sensory apparatus, let us simply achieve the greater reward of *seeing* the Andromeda galaxy rather than comprehending the exact vastness of its distance. To do so, pick a clear, dark night in late summer or fall, and find the Great Square of Pegasus (see page 133). The star at the northeast corner of the Great Square, the one closest to the north celestial pole and to the constellation Cassiopeia, is one of the few stars in the sky to be

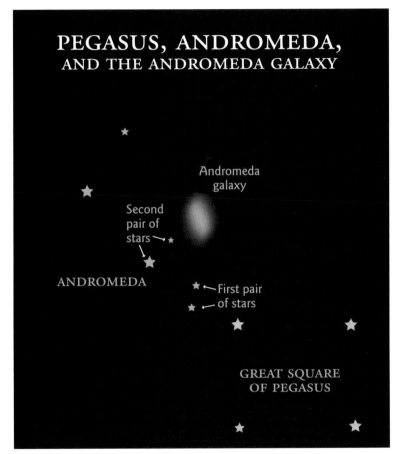

PEGASUS, ANDROMEDA,
AND THE ANDROMEDA GALAXY

Andromeda galaxy

Second pair of stars

ANDROMEDA

First pair of stars

GREAT SQUARE OF PEGASUS

To find the Andromeda galaxy, look for the pairs of stars that lie to the northeast of Pegasus. The second pair point toward the faint, fuzzy galaxy.

shared between two constellations, for it also forms the brightest star in Andromeda. We may call this the guide star for finding the Andromeda galaxy, though in fact its name is Alpheratz, a corruption of a longer Arabic name. The constellation Andromeda consists of two roughly parallel lines of not-so-bright stars, with three stars in each line, that extend from this guide star to the northeast, in roughly the direction of Cassiopeia. Since three stars appear in each of these lines, the two lines may be seen as three pairs of stars as you direct your gaze from the guide star in the Great Square to the region immediately below Cassiopeia. The pairs of stars at progressively greater distances from the guide star show a progressively wider spacing between their stars, and in each of these pairs the southern star (the one farther from Cassiopeia) shines a bit more brightly than the northern one.

Take your time in finding these two lines of stars. When you feel confident that you have them in view, turn your attention to the second pair outward from the guide star. Move your gaze from the southern (lower) star through the northern (upper) one in this pair, and extend that line for the same distance as that separating the two stars. There you will find the haze of the

Andromeda galaxy, covering an area larger than the full moon, but nowhere as bright. To be sure that you have found the galaxy, look at it not directly but with your averted vision, where your eyes have greater sensitivity (a highly useful trait evolved in the days when our enemies attacked from the side). Have you indeed found the fuzzy patch of sky, the light from 200 billion stars that must have traveled for more than two million years to reach your eyes? Is it still there? Can you verify that the shape of this fuzziness resembles that of an ellipse, with its long axis roughly parallel to the two lines of stars in Andromeda? Then you have joined the club, with a membership far less numerous than you might expect, of those who can point to the sky and correctly say, "*There* you see another full galaxy of stars, something like our own Milky Way."

MEDITATION

We have reached the end of our tour of the heavens, finished for now with the nine ways for you to connect with the universe. This might be an appropriate spot to reflect on the difference between seeing what you *ought* to see and seeing for yourself, a division of labor well illustrated by finding the Andromeda galaxy.

If you performed that activity well, you have (I hope!) followed my directions in finding first the Great Square of Pegasus, then the two chains of stars in Andromeda, then the galaxy itself, marked by the two stars in those chains that can be used as pointers toward this object. Do you realize that in finding the Andromeda galaxy, you saw an object that millions of our ancestors saw—yet never truly noted? So far as we can tell, no early astronomers, no matter how skilled, in China, Japan, India, Mesopotamia, Egypt, the Americas, or Europe ever noticed this fuzzy patch of light, at least to the point of recording it as worthy of description. When Johannes Bayer drew the first modern star atlas in 1603, he made a fine representation of the stars in Andromeda, some of which shine nowhere nearly so brightly as the galaxy; yet you can search back and forth over this map without finding a hint of the galaxy.

How could this be so? The Andromeda galaxy has not changed its brightness, human eyes have grown no better at perceiving faint objects, and the night sky has hardly grown darker since ancient times. It seems clear that ancient astronomers failed to record the Andromeda galaxy because they had no place for it in their minds. The milky way formed a coherent band of light around the sky, but the single fuzzy cloud of the galaxy in Andromeda had no role to play in the way that humans conceived the cosmos. Consequently they ignored it, so far as we can tell. Could it be that some astronomers asked themselves and their colleagues, "Don't you see a glow over there above the Great Square?" If so, their colleagues and their psyches presumably answered, "Nonsense! That makes no sense at all!"

Long eras had to pass before we accepted the notion that our picture of the heavens could be wrong. In the sixteenth century, Tycho Brahe observed a new comet and a new star in the sky, and demonstrated that both of these objects must be farther away than the moon, and must therefore form part of the "unchanging" spheres of heaven. Even so, Tycho's news took a long time to sink in. And Tycho, the finest astronomical observer the pre-telescopic world ever saw, never mentioned the Andromeda galaxy.

So ask yourself, "What would I have made of the fuzzy patch of light had I happened to see it on a clear dark night? How could I have learned what this object might be, or if indeed this fuzzy light comes from a cosmic object at all?" I have a prejudice, of course, in favor of your consulting reference works such as this one, but an even greater desire to see minds roam free, asking the question, Why do I believe these things that experts tell me? I don't mean to imply that you should never, or even rarely, believe scientific expertise, but the question should always come to the forefront of your mind. Now that you know how to connect with the universe, you can better understand the long road of error and confusion, clarity and comprehension, that humans have followed to reach our present state of awareness about the cosmos. May it increase—and may you bring a positive, healthy, and organized skepticism to bear on those who tell you why things are the way they are.

APPENDIX A: FURTHER READING

Allen, Richard Hinckley. *Star Names: Their Lore and Meaning*. New York: Dover Publications, 1963.

Branley, Franklyn. *Experiments in Sky Watching*. New York: Thomas Y. Crowell, 1959.

Chartrand, Mark. *National Audubon Society Field Guide to the Night Sky*. New York: Alfred A. Knopf, 1991.

Harrison, Edward. *Darkness at Night: A Riddle of the Universe*. Cambridge, MA: Harvard University Press, 1987.

Holmes, Hannah. *The Secret Life of Dust: From the Cosmos to the Kitchen Counter, the Big Consequences of Little Things*. New York: John Wiley & Sons, 2001.

Krupp, Edwin. *Beyond the Blue Horizon: Myths and Legends of the Sun, Moon, Stars, and Planets*. New York: Harper Collins, 1991.

Krupp, Edwin. *Echoes of the Ancient Skies: The Astronomy of Lost Civilizations*. New York: Harper & Row, 1983.

Kyselka, Will, and Ray Lanterman. *North Star to Southern Cross*. Honolulu: University Press of Hawaii, 1974.

Nininger, H. H. *Out of the Sky: An Introduction to Meteorites*. New York: Dover Books, 1952.

Rey, H. A. *The Stars: A New Way to See Them*. Boston: Houghton Mifflin, 1952.

Whitney, Charles. *Whitney's Star Finder*. New York: Alfred A. Knopf, 1974.

APPENDIX B: ASTRONOMY INTERNET WEBSITES

I list below some of the URLs for internet websites that deal with observational astronomy as well as with related topics such as the search for life in the universe. This list is, of course, by no means exhaustive. Each of these sites typically contains links to many other sites, thus offering the chance to explore the cosmos ever more deeply.

Website	URL
Astronomy Picture of the Day	http://antwrp.gsfc.nasa.gov/apod/astropix.html
Pictures from NASA and the Jet Propulsion Laboratory	http://www.jpl.nasa.gov/pictures/
Ask an Astronomer	http://itss.raytheon.com/cafe/qadir/qanda.html
Observational astronomy links	http://www.earth.uni.edu/astro/obs.html
Sun Moon and Stars	http://www.infoplease.com/spot/sunmoondec01.html
	(Change the month and year in this URL from "dec01" to the desired month and year)
The Nine Planets	http://seds.lpl.arizona.edu/billa/tnp/nineplanets.html
Powers of Ten	http://powersof10.com
Amateur astronomy observing	http://www.e-z.net/~haworth/index.html
Planets around other stars	http://www.exoplanets.org
	http://www.obspm.fr/encycl/catalog.html
SETI (The Search for Extraterrestrial Intelligence)	http://www.seti-inst.edu/
	http://seti.berkeley.edu/
The Astrobiology Web	http://www.astrobiology.com/extreme.html
Scifi/Science	http://www.niac.usra.edu
Bad Astronomy in Movies	http://www.badastronomy.com

PHOTO CREDITS

Cover Photo
Courtesy of Masterfile
Page iv Photograph by Donald Goldsmith

Chapter One
Page 1 Courtesy of David K. Lynch
Page 4 Photograph by Donald Goldsmith
Page 11 Courtesy of Richard Cooper
Page 16 Courtesy of Dick Fritts

Chapter Two
Page 21 NASA photograph
Page 24 Courtesy of Photodisc/NASA
Page 39 Photograph by Donald Goldsmith
Page 42 Photograph by Donald Goldsmith

Chapter Three
Page 45 Courtesy of David Morrison

Chapter Four
Page 61 Courtesy of United States Naval Observatory
Page 67 Courtesy of Jerry Schad

Chapter Five
Page 79 Courtesy of Juan Carlos Casado
Page 88 Courtesy of Jerry Schad

Chapter Six
Page 95 Photograph by Donald Goldsmith
Page 115 Courtesy of Woodruff T. Sullivan III

Chapter Seven
Page 117 Courtesy of Frank Zullo
Page 131 Courtesy of Jerry Schad

Chapter Eight
Page 141 NASA photograph
Page 156 Courtesy of Jerry Schad
Page 160 NASA photograph
Page 162 Courtesy of Corbis Images

Chapter Nine
Page 165 Courtesy of Rick Scott and Joe Orman
Page 168 Courtesy of Frank Zullo
Page 171 Courtesy of Jerry Schad
Page 179 Courtesy of Roger Smith/NOAO/AURA/NSF

Appendix B
Page 185 Courtesy of Corbis Images

All diagrams and illustrations
By Donald Goldsmith and Tressa Minervini

About the Author

Donald Goldsmith has written more than a dozen books about astronomy, cosmology, and space science, including *The Hunt for Life on Mars*, *The Runaway Universe*, and *The Astronomers*, which was the companion book to the PBS series. The American Astronomical Society presented him with a lifetime achievement award for his efforts to make astronomy popular and interesting.